Clarendon Press Series

A

HISTORICAL GRAMMAR

OF THE

FRENCH TONGUE

BY

AUGUSTE BRACHET

TRANSLATED BY

G. W. KITCHIN, M. A.

Oxford

AT THE CLARENDON PRESS

MDCCCLXIX

PREFACE.

THIS Historical Grammar, which proposes to study the laws of formation of the French tongue, is not meant to swell the list of those purely grammatical works whose object is to facilitate the practical acquirement of the language.

For it is no longer sufficient simply to regard the study of language as an useful preparation for the study of literature. It is now seen that speech, which belongs alike to all the human race, must, like all natural phenomena, follow fixed laws, and pass in its transformations through regular stages. Linguistic studies may, therefore, be an end in themselves; for instead of pursuing them in a spirit of idle curiosity, we may investigate the manner in which the law of change, which governs all nature, is applied to languages.

It is an old saying that languages are not born but transmuted: philology investigates the law of this transmutation, using for her instruments history and comparison. Let us explain:—in those sciences which are based on observation, such as chemistry or natural history, it is impossible to account for any fact unless we know what fact preceded it: if we would explain how a tree is formed, we must go back from tree to young shoot, from shoot to germ or seed; in other words, we must make out the history of the tree by careful observation of the different conditions and forms through which it has passed. We best discern that which is by knowing that which has been; the right way to discover the causes of any phenomenon is to look at the same time at those phenomena which have preceded it. So too for philology, which is, if we may hazard the phrase, the botany of language; here also we may best explain words or grammatical facts by the study of their history. A single example will put this in a clearer light.

It is well known that before certain feminine substances, such as *messe, mère, soif, faim, peur*, &c., the adjective *grand* keeps its masculine termination, *grand'messe, grand'mère*, &c. Why so? Grammarians, who are puzzled by nothing, tell us without hesitation that *grand* is here put for *grande*, and that the apostrophe marks the suppression of the final *e*. But the good sense of every scholar protests against this: after having learnt in childhood that *e* mute is cut off before a vowel, and never before a consonant, he is told that the *e* is here cut off without the slightest reason in such phrases as *grand'route*, &c. The real explanation is in fact a very different one. In its beginning, French grammar was simply the continuation and prolongation of Latin grammar; consequently the Old French adjectives followed in all points the Latin adjective; those adjectives which had two terminations for masculine and feminine in Latin (as **bonus, bona**) had two in Old French, whereas those Latin adjectives which had but one (as **grandis, fortis**, &c.), had only one in French. In the thirteenth century men said *une grand femme*, **grandis femina**; *une âme mortel*, **mortalis anima**; *une coutume cruel*, **crudelis**; *une plaine vert*, **viridis planities**, &c. In the fourteenth century the meaning of this distinction was no longer understood; and men, deeming it a mere irregularity, altered the form of the second to that of the first class of adjectives, and wrote *grande*, *verte*, *forte*, &c., after the pattern of *bonne*, &c. A trace of the older and more correct form survives in such expressions as *grand'mère*, *grand'route*, *grand'faim*, *grand'-garde*, &c., which are the *débris* of the older language. In the seventeenth century, Vaugelas and the grammarians of the age, in their ignorance of the historic reason of this usage, pompously decreed that the form of these words arose from an *euphonic* suppression of the *e* mute, which must be indicated by an apostrophe.

Here then is a natural explanation founded on history; and even if historical grammar had no other results beyond that of rendering ordinary grammars more logical and simple, it would still be worth much. But instead of employing this clear and fruitful method of observation, instead of studying the past to get a better understanding of the present, all our grammarians, from Vaugelas to M. Girault-Duvivier, have limited themselves to the study of the language in its actual form, and have tried to explain *à priori* (by pure reason and logic) facts which can be explained only by the history of our language and the study of its ancient state. And accordingly, for the last three centuries, they have built up systems which were both learned and puerile, intead of limiting themselves to the simple observation of facts ; they persist in treating philology as Voltaire treated geology, when he affirmed that the shells found on mountain-tops had been dropped there by pilgrims on their return from the crusades. The severe judgement passed by an eminent professor at the College of France[1] on French grammarians is fully justified : — 'La

---

[1] M. Bréal, *Discours d'ouverture du cours de grammaire comparée au Collége de France,* 1864.

grammaire traditionnelle formule ses prescriptions comme les décrets d'une volonté aussi impénétrable que décousue ; la philologie comparée fait glisser dans ces ténèbres un rayon de bon sens, et au lieu d'une docilité machinale elle demande à l'élève une obéissance raisonnable.'

I have illustrated by one example the position that these grammatical facts must be explained by an appeal to history, and that 'the present state of an idiom is but the natural consequence of its previous state, which alone makes it intelligible.' The same is true of words : given, for example, the word *âme*, we will seek for its origin. Before we come to any conclusion, let us see whether the history of the word (i. e. the study of the several forms it has successively taken) can throw any light on the problem, and shew us which path to follow. The accent on the *a* shews that some letter has been suppressed : in thirteenth-century texts, the word is written *anme;* in the eleventh century it is *aneme;* in the tenth *anime*, which leads us without a moment's hesitation to *anima*. Thus is history the guiding-line of philology, and there is not a single broken link in the long chain which connects the French with the Latin language.

When we first look at it, the distance between *âme* and *anima*, between the French of Voltaire and the peasant Latin, seems long enough; and yet it has needed only a series of infinitely small changes spread over a very long period to connect them with one another. Nature, wasteful of time, is sparing of effort; with slow and almost imperceptible modifications she arrives at results far away in appearance from her starting-point[1].

---

[1] M. G. Paris.

To history, regarded as an instrument of philology, comparison must be added as a precious ally. By comparison theories are proved, hypotheses verified. Thus, in the example we have already cited, the comparison of the Italian and Spanish *alma* with the French *âme* gives to the hypothesis we have started an invincible certainty.

Armed with this double method, the historical and the comparative, an illustrious German, Frederick Diez, wrote (A.D. 1836 to 1842) a comparative grammar of the five languages which spring from Latin[1]: he shewed according to what laws they were formed from the Latin. Starting from the philological principles laid down by him, Bartsch and Mätzner in Germany, and in France Littré, Guessard, P. Meyer, and G. Paris, have applied his principles to the French language in particular, and by means of many detailed investigations have thrown fresh light upon its origin[2].

---

[1] The Germans call these five (Italian, Spanish, French, Portuguese, Wallachian) the Romance languages; the name is clear and convenient, has been fully accepted in scientific language, and will be employed throughout this book.

[2] The work of these French philologers is far from being equally good: to say nothing of the very unequal compilation published by M. Ampère, or of M. Chevallet's book, an admirable work in its day, but now out of date, we must regard with real sorrow the success which welcomed twenty years ago M. Génin's work (*Variations de la langue française*), a collection of paradoxes and startling effects, performed by a juggler with words, whose business it is to astonish a dazzled audience. M. Génin was clever enough to know that his French readers would always prefer a well-turned epigram to a dry truth, and though he had never in his life read a single line of German, he was ever ready with a pleasantry—rather stale perhaps, but still always applauded in France—on 'the nebulous lucubrations of German brains.' He forgot that a *bon mot* does not do for an argument, and that in scientific matters it is no question of French or German ideas, but of right and wrong ones.

In.spite of these incessant efforts, the principles of French philology, scarcely recognised even by the learned, are still utterly unknown to the great majority of the literary public. My aim in this little book is to spread the knowledge of these results by freeing them from their scientific dress, and by making them accessible to a wider circle of readers. I have accordingly endeavoured to gather into a small volume the chief laws which have guided the formation of the French tongue. This is the only novelty I have to offer : for such works are not uncommon, at any rate outside of France. In Germany and England the study of the mother-tongue has won its citizenship in colleges and schools, where it has its undisputed seat by the side of Greek and Latin[1]; it has not as yet penetrated into French colleges, even as a branch of higher education.

M. Fourtoul, who, among a number of mistakes, hit on several happy discoveries, ordered in 1853 that comparative grammar should be taught in the upper classes of the Lyceum—a step towards the study of the French language which was reversed by his successor. This is much to be regretted, especially since the present ministry, which has ceased to insist on the study of Greek and Latin, and has established industrial or technical education side by side with literary training, ought all the more to have strengthened the latter by introducing the study of the three languages,

---

[1] It will be enough to cite two elementary works, whose numerous editions prove their success: in England, Gleig's *History of the English Language*, in his *School Series ;* in Germany, Vilmar's *German Historical Grammar*, intended for the higher forms in the Gymnasia (*Anfangsgründe der deutschen Grammatik, zunächst für die obersten Klassen der Gymnasien.* v. Dr. Vilmar. 6te Auflage, 1864).

Greek, Latin, and French, together with that of the three national literatures.

One Frenchman, M. Monjean, Director of the Chaptal College, has ventured to introduce a course of lectures on the history of the French language in his rhetoric class, with the very best results. May his example embolden the University of Paris to spread among the higher classes of our schools the results which have been indisputably obtained by science ! My object will have been gained if my modest manual of philology can in any way hasten this result.

I cannot hope to set forth a complete historical grammar in two hundred pages, when three volumes would scarcely suffice. I have therefore laid aside all secondary matters and points of detail, and have thought it enough to set forth essential laws and fundamental principles, so as not to overstep the limits of space which I had imposed on myself.

Again, the subject of this book is not the grammar of Old French. The French language in its mediæval state finds a place in it only so far as it illustrates Modern French (if I may apply to my little book what M. Littré said of his Historical Dictionary). Present usage depends on ancient usage, and can only be explained by it. Modern French without Old French is a tree without roots; Old French by itself is a tree without branches or leaves : the separation of the two is an injustice to both—an injustice constantly done to them up to the present time ; and their proper combination is the only originality claimed for this book, and gives it a right to be called a Historical Grammar.

The book is in three distinct parts : first, the Introduction, which sketches the history of the French language, of its formation, and of its elements ; secondly, the Historical Grammar, which deals with the Letters (Book I), Inflexion (Book II), and the Formation of Words (Book III) ; and lastly, an Appendix containing the rules to be followed in the discovery of etymologies.

Finally, I must express my gratitude to MM. Egger, Littré, and Ernest Renan, Members of the Institute, who have kindly given me the advantage of their advice and encouragement; to M. Émile Lemoine, formerly pupil of the École Polytechnique ; last of all and most of all, to MM. Paul Meyer and G. Paris, whose friendship has strengthened me for my task. If this book has any value, it is to them that it is due.

AUGUSTE BRACHET.

May 6, 1867.

[The present English edition has had throughout the great benefit of the counsel and oversight of Professor Max Müller, to whom hearty thanks are due for the interest he has taken in its welfare.

There are a few Latin words in the work marked with an asterisk, as **testonem** * ; these are late and unclassical.]

CONTENTS.

BOOK I.

Phonetics, or the study of the Letters.

PART I. *Permutation of Letters.*

BOOK II.

Inflexion, or the study of Grammatical Forms.

PART I. *Declension.*

BOOK III.

Formation of Words.

CORRIGENDA.

Page 11, line 2, *for* the Fat, *read* the Simple.

" 50, " 21, *omit* n.

" 51, " 9, *transpose the paragraph* From a primitive n.. .con-
stare, *to line* 21.

" " " 15, *after* i, *add* n.

" 103, " 16, *for* course, *read* cursus.

" " " 25, *for* clypeus buccularius, *read* scutum buccu-
larium.

" 106, " 20, *for* triginti, *read* triginta.

" 154, " 26, *for* aliorsam, *read* aliorsum.

INTRODUCTION.

I.

HISTORY OF THE FRENCH LANGUAGE.

CAESAR tells us that he found in Gaul three races, differing in speech, manners, and laws: the Belgae in the north, the Aquitani between the Garonne and the Pyrenees, and in the centre the Gallic or Celtic race. But the Belgae and the Celts really belonged to the same race, while the Aquitani were partly Iberian, and their language has perhaps survived in the Basque or *Euskarian* tongue.

Thus, then, almost all the soil of France was occupied by the Celtic race; they were men tall and fair, eager for excitement and noise, whose ambition was to fight well and to speak well.

Some six hundred years before the Christian era Marseilles (Massilia) was founded near the mouths of the Rhone by Phocaean refugees. This city, thanks to her relations with Rome, was destined to be the beginning of woes to the people of Gaul. She called in the Romans to defend her against the Ligurians in B.C. 153. The Romans seized the Rhone valley; and thence, in Caesar's time, passed on to conquer the rest of the land. The Celts resisted bravely: Caesar broke their spirit only by the most cruel measures; he massacred ten thousand women and children at Bourges;

B

slew the heads of a tribe at Vannes, and sold the rest by auction; cut off his prisoners' hands at Uxellodunum. After eight years of this work Gaul was subdued, and Rome began to administer her conquest.

The chief secret of Roman foreign politics lay in the perfection of her iron system of colonisation. She had two engines by which to hold down a conquered province, —her military colonies set all round the frontier, so as to isolate the conquest from all external influences; and then, secondly, an energetic 'administration' within that circle which soon broke up all local resistance. The language and religion of the conqueror was forced on the subject: all resistance was crushed by extermination or deportation; the vacuum filled up with colonists and freedmen from Rome.

By this method conquerors and conquered were in a few years completely welded into one mass. Less than a century after the conquest, Latin was spoken in many parts of Gaul. But this Latin, brought in by colonists and soldiers, was very unlike the Latin of Virgil: it was distinguished from the classical or written Latin by peculiarities of vocabulary and of inflexion which demand our attention.

It is a first law of history that all languages (just like the nations that use them), are one at first, but presently split into two parts—the speech of the noble and that of the people. Every language has its epoch of division: it comes when the nation opens its eyes to arts and poetry, in a word, to culture and literature. From that time the nation may be divided into two great classes, the lettered and the unlettered.

The Latin language underwent this same division at the time of the second Punic war. The separation increased as time went on. Greek art and Greek manners introduced into the literary language of Rome a crowd of purely Greek words utterly unknown to the popular idiom[1]. These words, marks of breeding, but servile copies of the Greek, remained as strange to the common people, as the aristocratic French-English terms, 'turf,' 'sport,' 'steeple-chase, &c., or the technical terms of science, 'diluvium,' 'stratification,' 'ornithology,' &c., are to the French peasantry at the present day. These borrowed words widened the breach between the literary and the popular Latin, a difference which ever increased, until the 'sermo nobilis,' the literary, aristocratic, 'classical' Latin, became in Caesar's day entirely distinct from the 'sermo plebeius, rusticus,' the 'castrense verbum,' as authors disdainfully styled it, the Latin of the people and the camp.

Each had its own grammatical forms and vocabulary. For example, 'to strike' is **verberare** in literary Latin; the popular Latin said **batuere**: the French words, *cheval, semaine, aider, doubler, bataille,* &c., were, in the classical Latin, **equus, hebdomas, juvare, duplicare, pugna**; in the popular, **cabállus, septimána, adjutáre, dupláre, batuália.**

The popular Latin was unwritten, and we might have remained ignorant of its existence had not the Roman grammarians revealed it to us by exhorting their students to avoid as low and trivial certain expressions which, they tell us, were in common vulgar use. Cassiodorus tells us that the feigned combats of gladiators and exercise-drill of the army were called **batalia**, 'Quae *vulgo* **batalia** dicuntur, exercitationes gladiatorum vel militum significant.' **Pugna** was the literary term, **batalia** the popular; **pugna** has disappeared, **batalia** has survived in *bataille.* The pedants of that day could not foresee that the literary idiom, which they admired so much, would one day disappear; and that

---

[1] As ἀμφιθέατρον, ἱππόδρομος, ἐφίππιον, φιλοσοφία, γεωγραφία, &c.

the popular Latin would reign in its room, parent of Italian, French, and Spanish, and strong enough to bear the weight of the literatures of three powerful nations.

Imported into Gaul by soldiers and colonists, the popular idiom soon made itself at home, and, even in the first century of the Christian era, had supplanted the Celtic speech, except in Armorica and a few isolated spots[1]. A hundred years after the conquest, women and children used to sing Latin songs; and so universal became the use of the language, that in Strabo's time the Celt was no longer regarded as a Barbarian[2]. The lengthy sojourn of the Legions, the incessant influx of colonists, the necessity of pleading in Latin before the Roman tribunals, the conversion of the people to Christianity, and lastly, the natural vivacity and love of change[3] which distinguishes the Celt, were further causes which contributed to the adoption by the Gallic people of the language of their conquerors.

But, at the same time that the people thus accepted the common Latin, the upper classes in Gaul were ambitious to adopt the literary dialect, practised rhetoric, and hoped to rise to political distinctions. From the days of Augustus, Gaul became a nursery for rhetoricians and grammarians; the schools of Autun, Bordeaux, and Lyons were renowned throughout the Empire. Pliny boasts that his works were known throughout Gaul[4]. Caesar admitted Celts to the Senate; Claudius enabled them to undertake all public offices, on the sole condition that they knew Latin. It is easy to understand why the Celtic noble forgot his mother-tongue.

---

[1] The Celtic lingered long after this date in Auvergne.

[2] That is, the test of language (implied in the word Barbarian) placed the Gaul on the same footing with the average Roman colonist.

[3] See Caes. B. G. 4. 5.

[4] Pliny, Ep. 9. 2.

That tongue disappeared, leaving a few faint traces as evidences that it had existed. Thus the Romans remarked that the bird they called galerita was called alauda in Gaul ; that 'beer,' in Graeco-Latin zythum, was cervisia in Gallic : they introduced the words into their own tongue, and these new Latin words, passing six centuries later into French, produced the words *alouette* [1] and *cervoise.* These and a few other isolated words, together with certain names of places, are all that the French language owes to the Gallic ; and indeed, if we speak more exactly, the French has borrowed nothing from it, since these words have passed through an intermediate Latin stage, and are not directly introduced into French from Gallic. But these cases are so very rare, that it may almost be affirmed that the influence of Celtic upon French has been inappreciable.

Thus, while the French nation is really Celtic in race, its language is not so : a very remarkable fact, which shews, better than any history could do, what a strong absorbent was the Roman power.

The Celtic language had scarcely accepted its defeat[2], when the Latin, from this time forth the true mistress of

---

[1] Alauda did not pass directly into *alouette*, but into the O.Fr. *aloue*, of which *alouette* is the diminutive.

[2] The Celtic language, thrust by the Romans back into Armorica, survived there for centuries, and was revived by an immigration of Kymri from Wales in the seventh century. The Bretons resisted the Frank as successfully as they had withstood the Roman; and what is now called the Low Breton patois is the direct descendent of the Celtic language. It has a considerable literature of tales, songs, and plays, which, however, only date back as far as the fourteenth century. But the language, living thus for a thousand years 'in extremis,' naturally has deviated far from the primitive Celtic tongue : for beside the natural corruption and degradation of eighteen centuries, it has been forced to admit into its ranks a crowd of foreign, that is, of French, terms ; and consequently many Breton words present the singular spectacle of having two distinct forms, the one

Gaul, had to enter on a fresh struggle, and to repel a new assailant. The invasion of the German tribes set in. As far back as the second century after Christ the barbarians began slowly to filter through into the Gaelic soil: they silently undermined the dykes of the Roman Empire, and prepared for the bursting of the barriers, and the terrible inundations of the fifth century.

To protect northern Gaul against these German invasions, the Romans garrisoned their frontiers with a chain of legions or military colonies; and when these veterans were no longer able to defend the sanctity of the Roman territory, the Romans employed an expedient which kept the great invasion at bay for a whole century, and for a few years at least gave peace to the Empire. They determined to let the barbarians settle in Northern Gaul, to attach them to the Empire, and to use them as a new and durable barrier against all further invasions. These were the **Leti**[1], colonies of barbarians who recognised the nominal sovereignty of the Emperors, and enjoyed lands granted them

---

ancient and of Celtic origin, the other more modern, borrowed from the French, but modified by a Celtic termination. Thus in Breton we have for

just	*egwirion*	or *just,*
secretly	*ekuz*	or *secretament,*
troubled	*enkrezet*	or *troublet,*
anger	*buanégez*	or *coler,* and so on.

Here the middle column is composed of old Celtic words; the third of corrupted French words. It would not have been necessary to insist on so elementary a truth, had not a theory been started in the eighteenth century that these Celtic importations were really the origin of the French language. Le Brigant and the well-known La Tour d'Auvergne supported this opinion. Voltaire called this etymological folly Celto-mania: its believers amused the world by extravagant assertions—that Celtic was the original speech of Paradise; that Adam, Eve, the old serpent, all spoke Low Breton. These errors have had a still worse result; for they have cast unmerited discredit on all Celtic studies.

[1] Probably a form of the German word *leute.* See Du Cange.

under a kind of military tenure. At the same time the Emperors hired Franks, Burgundians, Alans, to fill up the blanks in their legions.

The consequence was an ever-increasing introduction of German words into the common Latin ; these terms, as was natural, being chiefly connected with warfare. Vegetius, in his 'De re militari,' tells us that the Roman soldiers gave the name of **burgus** to a fortified work[1]. This is the German *Burg*. Thus, nearly a century before Clovis, German terms had got into the Latin language : it is clear that after the German invasion this influence will greatly increase in strength.

But we must first note down the chief features of the Latin of the last ages of the Empire. A century after the Roman conquest Gaul was flourishing and prosperous. The Latin language in its two forms pursued a tranquil course— the common dialect in cities and in the fields, the literary dialect among the aristocracy and middle classes. In the second century after Christ, the time of the highest splendour of Roman Gaul, the popular dialect was in the shade, while literary Latin shone with great brilliancy ; the Gallic schools produced lawyers and rhetoricians : and Juvenal calls Gaul ' nutricula causidicorum.'

But in the fifth century, just before the German invasion, the scene is very different : the two dialects have changed places; literary Latin is dying; the popular dialect spreads widely, and this even before the invasion of A.D. 407. The institution of the 'Curials' in the cities, and the extinction of the older municipal bodies, gave its deathblow to literature and the literary dialect. The better classes perished, schools were everywhere shut up, literary culture came to an immediate stop, and ignorance speedily recovered all the ground

---

[1] ' Castellum parvum, quod **burgum** vocant.'

she had lost. From this time the use of the written Latin, a dialect which only lived in books and by tradition, was confined to the Gallo-Roman nobles, a handful of men who transmitted to their children a petrified idiom, which had no life, and was destined to perish with them, when their time came. And here again popular Latin won by the losses of the literary dialect.

At last the Roman Empire fell under the attacks of the barbarians. In the whirlwind, administration, justice, aristocracy, literature, all perished, and with them the language[1]

---

[1] M. Meyer says well that 'the invasion of the barbarians irrevocably fixed the gulf between these two idioms, between the common Latin, the mistress of Gaul, ready to be the mother of the French language, and the literary dialect, a dead language, used only by the learned, and destined to have no influence in the formation of modern languages. This dialect was kept up by Gregory of Tours, Fredegarius, the literary renaissance under Charlemagne, and by scholasticism; it was perpetuated in learned use, and in the sixteenth century experienced, after the great renaissance, a kind of artificial resurrection. Even in our own day it is the official language of the Roman Catholic Church, and, until quite lately, was the language of the learned, especially in Germany.'

After the invasion under the Merovingian kings, the public personages, notaries or clergy, too ignorant to write literary Latin correctly, too proud to use the common Latin in their documents, and eager to imitate the fine style of Roman officials, wrote 'a sort of jargon, which is neither literary Latin nor popular Latin, but a strange mixture of both, with the common dialect more or less preponderant, according to the ignorance of the writer.' This jargon is what is called Low Latin. It continued to be the language of the French administration up to 1539, when Francis I ordered French to be used in all public acts. This distinction between *Low Latin,* a gross and barren imitation of the Roman literary dialect, and *Popular Latin,* the living language of the people, and parent of the French tongue, must not be forgotten. It should be added that there is, besides, a second kind of Low Latin, that of the middle ages, which reproduced French words in a servile way: as for example, **missaticum** produced the French *message;* and again *message* was retranslated into **messagium.**

which they had employed. Then the common dialect entirely supplanted the other. If proof of this were needed, we should find it in the fact that wherever the literary and the common dialect used two different words for the same thing, the French language has invariably taken the latter, and thrown aside the former: an absolute proof that the literary dialect was confined to the upper classes, and flourished and perished with them. Illustrations are innumerable. thus—

LITERARY LATIN.	POPULAR LATIN.	FRENCH.
Hebdomas	septimana	*semaine*
		(O.Fr. *sepmaine*)
Equus	caballus	*cheval*
Verberare	batuere	*battre*
Pugna	battalia	*bataille*
Osculari	basiare	*baiser*
Iter	viaticum	*voyage*
Verti	tornare	*tourner*
Urbs	villa	*ville*
Os	bucca	*bouche*
Felis	catus	*chat*
Duplicare	duplare	*doubler*
Sinere	laxare	*laisser*
Tentamen	exagium	*essai*
Gulosus	glutonem	*glouton*
Jus	directus (drictus)	*droit*
Minae	minaciae	*menace*
Edere	manducare	*manger*
Ignis	focus	*feu*
Ludus	jocus	*jeu*
Aula	curtem	*cour*, &c.

These examples shew how incorrect it is to say that

French is classical Latin corrupted by an intermixture of popular forms; it is, on the contrary, the popular Latin alone.   The same is true wherever the invasion of the barbarians also destroyed the literary dialect.   Italian, Spanish, Portuguese, are the products of the slow development of the common Roman speech.   Hence the striking family likeness often noticed between these sister-tongues—

> ' Facies non omnibus una,
> Nec diversa tamen, qualem decet esse sororum.'

The German destroyed the literary dialect; but the common Latin was the gainer: eventually it succeeded in absorbing even its conquerors; it compelled them to forget their own language, and to adopt that of their subjects.

There are many causes which led to this result: first, the numerical paucity of the Franks, a few bands of men, scarcely more than twelve thousand in all, in the midst of six millions of Gallo-Romans; next, if the Franks had not accepted the Latin, what would they have taken for their common tongue?   Each German tribe had its own dialect, Frankish, Burgundian, Gothic, &c.   But, lastly, the conversion of the Franks to Christianity, which, as it were, bound them over to learn Latin, may be reckoned as the special cause which made the adoption of the Latin a necessity.

So they all tried to learn Latin; and, less than a century after the invasion, Fortunatus, Bishop of Poitiers, congratulated Haribert on the great success of his efforts :

> ' Qualis es in propria docto sermone loquela
> Qui nos Romano vincis in eloquio ?'

At Strasburg in A.D. 842, Ludwig the German takes an oath in French in the presence of the army of Karl the Bald; a clear proof that the Karling soldiers no longer

understood German. In the next century, when Hrolf
swore fealty to Karl the Fat (A.D. 911), he had scarcely
begun the formula with 'Bi Got' (In the name of God)
when all the company of lords burst out laughing; so utterly
was German forgotten, that it actually sounded ridiculous
in their ears.

Thus the Latin supplanted the German : yet a great
number of German words were retained to designate those
new institutions which the Franks brought in with them,
such as *vassal, alleu, fief,* &c. All terms relating to political
or judicial functions, all titles in the feudal hierarchy, are
of German origin. The German words *mahal, bann, alôd,
skepeno, marahscalh, siniscalh,* &c., are formed by common
Latin into **mallum, bannum, alodium, scabinus, mari-
scallus, siniscallus,** &c., whence, several centuries later, they
passed into the French *mall, ban, alleu, échevin, maréchal,
sénéchal,* &c. Still more is this the case with war terms. ·
The Franks long kept to themselves, as a privileged class,
the warlike profession; and the Gallo-Romans accepted
the terms which their masters employed : as *halsberc, haubert; helm, heaume; heriberg, auberge; werra, guerre,* &c.
There are upwards of nine hundred such words which
passed from the German into Latin, and thence into French.
This invasion touched the vocabulary only : there are no
traces of German influence on French syntax.

Common Latin was greatly affected by this sudden inroad
of barbarous words : its vocabulary became less and less
like that of the literary dialect; its syntax still further widened
the breach. Those analytical tendencies which appear in
all modern languages, and which cause the use of prepositions
instead of inflected cases to mark *possession* and *aim,* soon
shewed themselves in popular Latin. The literary dialect
said, 'Do panem *Petro,*' or 'equus *Petri;*' but the popular
Latin said, 'Do panem *ad Petrum,*' 'caballus *de Petro :*' and

similarly auxiliaries were introduced in the conjugation of verbs[1]. Thus modified in its syntax, and augmented in its vocabulary, popular Latin became a really distinct language; and the men of culture in Merovingian times called it, slightingly, ' lingua romana rustica,' Peasant-Latin.

Its position as an independent language is attested early. Church writers give us the earliest proofs of it, as we should expect; for the Church, through her missionaries and her priests, first addressed the people, and in order to be understood, she must use their language. Thus, as early as A.D. 660, St. Mummolinus is elected Bishop of Noyon, because he can speak both German and Romance[2]. We read in the life of St. Adalhard, Abbot of Corby in A.D. 750, that he preached in the popular tongue 'with a sweet fluency;' and his biographer gives us clearly the distinction between the two dialects when he says, ' When St. Adalhard spoke the *common*, that is, the *Roman* tongue, you would have thought he knew no other; if he spoke German, he was still more brilliant; but if he used the *Latin*, he spoke even better than in either of the others[3].'

Thus in the lifetime of Karl the Great (as we see from this passage), the people understood no Latin, and the Church had taken to preaching and teaching in French. There has come to light by a fortunate chance a fragment of a glossary, called the ' Glosses of Reichenau[4],' and written

---

[1] See below, p. 123.

[2] ' Quia praevalebat non tantum in Teutonica, sed etiam in *Romana lingua.*'

[3] ' Qui si vulgari, id est, *Romana lingua*, loqueretur, omnium aliarum putaretur inscius; si vero *Teutonica*, enitebat perfectius; si *Latina*, in nulla omnino absolutius.'—*Acta Sanctorum*, i. 416.

[4] Discovered in 1863 by M. Holtzmann in a MS. in the Library at Reichenau.

about A.D. 768, which explains many of the difficult words of the Vulgate in the French of the period. The words are written in two columns; on the left the Latin (Vulgate), on the right the French: thus—

LATIN.	FRENCH (of the 8th cent.)	MODERN FRENCH.
Minas	*Manatces*	*Menaces*
Galea	*Helmo*	*Heaume*
Tugurium	*Cabanna*	*Cabane*
Singulariter	*Solamente*	*Seulement*
Caementarii	*Macioni*	*Maçons*
Sindones	*Linciolo*	*Linceul*
Sagma	*Soma*	*Somme*
&c.	&c.	

This most interesting fragment is the first written monument of the French language, eleven hundred years old. The translation into modern French, in the right hand column, shews at a glance the distance between this still unformed dialect and the French of the present day.

These Glosses also shew that the inhabitants of France spoke French in Karl's days; in fact, Karl himself found it necessary to learn the language of his subjects.

And while Eginhard, Alcuin, Angilbert, and all the cultivated class of that day affected to despise this half-formed *patois*, the Church, which had never been afraid of using this vulgar speech, quickly took in its whole importance, and instead of resisting it, and clinging to literary Latin, set herself to make a skilful use of the new movement. Hitherto she had but tolerated, or perhaps patronised, the study of this vulgar tongue by priests and missionaries; but towards the end of Karl's reign, she did more: she ordered the clergy to study it, seeing that the people no longer understood Latin. In A.D. 813 the Council of Tours bid all priests expound the Holy Scriptures in the 'Romance,' and the preachers to use the same in their pulpits.

Thus the Church recognised the existence of this new language, and confessed that Latin was dead and gone from among the people ; and, when once she had settled this point, she carried it out to its natural results with her habitual perseverance. After the Council of Tours, those of Rheims in A.D. 813, of Strasburg in A.D. 842, and of Arles in A.D. 851, renewed the order to preachers, until in fact the vulgar. tongue was everywhere substituted for the Latin. Thus it gained ground rapidly ; so much so that five-and-twenty years after Karl's death, it was used as the language of political negociation in the famous Oaths of Strasburg which Ludwig the German took to his brother, Karl the Bald, and Karl's army took to Ludwig the German, in March, A.D. 842. Nithard, the nephew of Karl the Great, has preserved them in his 'History of the Franks,' written about A.D. 843, at the command of Karl the Bald, whose intimate friendhe was.

I. Oath taken by Ludwig the German.

Old French.	*Modern French.*
Pro Deo amur, et pro christian poblo et nostro commun salvament, d'ist di en avant, in quant Deus savir et podir me dunat, si salvarai eo cist meon fradre Karlo et in adjudha et in cadhuna cosa, si cum om per dreit son fradra salvar dist, in o quid il mi altresi fazet; et ab Ludher nul plaid numquam	Pour l'amour de Dieu et pour le salut du peuple chrétien et notre commun salut, de ce jour en avant, autant que Dieu me donne savoir et pouvoir, je sauverai mon frère Charles et en aide et en chaque chose (ainsi qu'on doit, selon la justice, sauver son frère), à condition qu'il en fasse autant pour moi, et je

prindrai, qui meon vol cist meon fradre Karle in damno sit. | ne ferai avec Lothaire aucun accord qui, par ma volonté, porte préjudice à mon frère Charles ici présent.

II. Oath of the Soldiers of Karl the Bald.

Old French. | *Modern French.*

Si Lodhuwigs sagrament, que son fradre Karlo jurat, conservat, et Karlus meos sendra de sua part non los tanit, si io returnar non l'int pois, ne io, ne neuls cui eo returnar int pois, in nulla adjudha contra Lodhuwig nun li iv er. | Si Louis garde le serment qu'il a juré à son frère Charles, et que Charles mon maître, de son côté, ne le tienne pas, si je ne l'en puis détourner, ni moi, ni nul que j'en puis détourner, ne lui serai en aide contre Louis.

Next after the Reichenau Glosses, these oaths are the oldest monuments of the French language : and their value is incalculable for students of the linguistic origin of the Romance tongues ; for we here catch, as it were, the Latin language in the act of transformation into French. The importance of this will appear in the course of this book : it is sufficient to remark here that the Frankish army clearly had lost all knowledge of Latin or German ; otherwise the German Emperor, Ludwig, would never have taken oath to them in French.

From this time the vulgar tongue took, once and for all, the place of the Latin which the people no longer understood. In common use during the last two centuries, officially acknowledged by the Church in A.D. 813, and by the State in A.D. 842, it increased in importance, and soon broke out in poetry. In the ninth century there appears a poem in French verse, on the martyrdom of St. Eulalia ;

in the tenth century we find two short poems, the one on the Passion, the other on the life of St. Leger of Autun. These are the first poetic attempts of the language.

These two centuries, the ninth and tenth, in which the later Karlings came to a wretched end, seem at first sight barren and desolate; but they are in reality fertile in the beginnings of French national life: with that life comes a national language, poetry, and art. All these things sprang into being from the people, not from the kings. The pretentious chroniclers of the time describe the last moments of the decrepit Karling dynasty; they pass over and have not noticed how fresh a life, and what creative energy was beginning to reanimate what seemed to be the worn-out powers of society[1].

From the tenth century the French nation begins its real life · the invasions of the barbarians are over[2]. On the ruins of the Karling empire feudalism, a new form of social life half-way between ancient slavery and modern freedom, will flourish for six centuries.

As the use of the French speech increased, the knowledge of Latin diminished. Hugh Capet knew no language but French: when he had an interview with Otto II, the Emperor of Germany, who spoke Latin to him, he was

---

[1] This birth of the French language in a historical age well-known to us is of the highest importance: we learn from it how such languages as Latin and Greek (which we know only in their full age) came first into being. And when our histories relate in full the obscure quarrels and struggles of obscure princes, and give us no details respecting this great event, we see clearly that true history has not yet found its way into the school-room. See M. Littré, *Histoire de la Langue Française*, i. 260, and the *Revue des Deux Mondes*, Feb. 15, 1867.

[2] The last invasion ended with the establishment of the Northmen in north-western France. Their numbers were small: they forgot their own tongue, and adopted that of their subjects. A century after Hrolf's death Normandy was celebrated for the excellence of her French.

obliged to get one of the bishops to act as interpreter. Even in the monasteries Latin ceased to be used after the eleventh century; there were even numbers of priests who knew nothing but French.

Thus at last Latin was abandoned even by the upper classes: they had clung to it three centuries after it had died out of common use.

Forthwith there sprang up, between the eleventh and the thirteenth centuries, a thoroughly original poetical literature; graceful or brilliant lyrics, and high epics, like the 'Chanson de Roland,' were written, and became exceedingly popular in other countries as well as at home.

It is also worthy of notice that the French language in the thirteenth century and onwards, was well known and accepted by neighbouring nations. The Norman Conquest imposed French on England: in Germany Frederick II and his court were familiar with French poetry; in Italy French was generally known and used; Marco-Polo wrote his travels in it; Brunetto Latini, Dante's master, composed his 'Trésor de Sapience' in it, 'because the French is the most delectable and most common tongue.' From every quarter students flocked to the University of Paris, and mediæval Latin lines testify to the fact.

'Filii nobilium, dum sunt juniores,
Mittuntur in Franciam fieri doctores.'

It is time that we asked, What is this French language which Europe valued so highly in the thirteenth century?

It is a well-known fact that the first cause of phonetic changes and transformations of language lies in the structure of the vocal organs; or, in other words, in difference of pronunciation; and this again results from difference of race. Thus Latin, introduced into Italy, Gaul, and Spain, and spoken by three different races, each in its own way, gradually was decomposed, as we have seen, into ·

three corresponding languages. In Gaul, popular Latin fell
into the hands of two rival races, North and South, and
produced two distinct idioms, that of the South, or the
'Langue d'Oc,' and that of the North, called the 'Langue
d'Oil[1].' These curious names spring from the custom, not
uncommon in the middle ages, of designating languages by
the sign of affirmation; just as Dante calls Italian ' la lingua
di *si.*' The modern French *oui* was *oil* in the North, and
oc in the South of France.

The 'Langue d'Oil,' which prevailed in districts inhabited
by populations whose characteristic differences were strongly
marked (the Normans, Picards, Burgundians, &c., having
their own peculiarities of pronunciation), was broken up in
its turn into corresponding dialects.   There was no one
capital; each great feudal district was independent, with
its own political and literary life, its own tongue, manners,
and customs.

Thus in Normandy or Picardy all official acts and literary
works were in the Norman or Picard dialect; the dialect
of the Ile de France, or French, as it then was called, was
regarded in Normandy as almost a foreign language.

There were in the middle ages four principal dialects
of the 'Langue d'Oil'—Norman, Picard, Burgundian, and

---

[1] A line·drawn from La Rochelle to Grenoble will fairly
represent the frontiers of the two dialects; north of it we have
the ' Langue d'Oil,' south of it the ' Langue d'Oc.'

This 'Langue d'Oc,' or, as it is now more commonly called,
Provençal, from the chief district in which it obtained, was
developed alongside of the Northern dialect ; and in the twelfth
century was the parent of a brilliant lyrical literature.

The rivalry of North and South, which ended in the Albigensian
war, and the defeat of the South, destroyed this Provençal literature.   In A.D. 1272 Languedoc became French, and the French
dialect soon prevailed.   The Provençal, Languedoc, and Gascon
patois, which still remain in the South, are but the fragmentary
remains of this ' Langue d'Oc,' which was so brilliant a language
for two centuries.

French[1] (of the Ile de France) in the centre of the triangle formed by the other three. These four dialects, which were equal in power and influence, had such marked differences that even strangers were struck by it: Roger Bacon (who was in France in A.D. 1240), when seeking to shew in his 'Opus Majus' what the dialects of a language may be, chooses French as his example. 'The idioms of the same language vary in different districts, as is clearly the case in France, which has numerous varieties of idiom among the French, the Normans, the Picards, and the Burgundians; and what is correct speech in Picardy, is looked on as a barbarism by the Burgundians, and even by the French[2].'

These differences of dialect, as in the Greek language, did not touch the syntax, but only the forms of words: thus, for example, amabam became, in the twelfth century, *amève* in Burgundy, *amoie* in the Ile de France, and *amoue* in Normandy. This word shews us how Latin words shrank and became stiffer as they went northwards: they form a kind of sensitive thermometer, which falls as it goes farther from the South; and this, not 'per saltum,' but by gradual change. May we not conclude that words, like plants, are modified by climate, which is one of the *factors* of language, as mathematicians say?

In the middle ages, these four dialects (like the four Greek dialects, Ionian, Aeolian, Attic, and Dorian) produced four distinct literatures: we can immediately distinguish a Norman from a French or a Burgundian writer. Each of these

---

[1] 'Frenchman,' in the middle ages, was exclusively the name of the inhabitant of the Ile de France.

[2] 'Nam et idiomata variantur ejusdem linguae apud diversos, sicut patet de *lingua Gallicana* quae apud *Gallicos*, et *Normannos*, et *Picardos*, et *Burgundos* multiplici variatur idiomate. Et quod propriè dicitur in idiomate Picardorum horrescit apud Burgundos, imo apud Gallicos viciniores.' Roger Bacon, *Opus Majus*, iii. 44.

languages had a separate and complete existence: we have
now to see how the four were reduced to one, and why
the dialect of the Ile de France was adopted as the common
tongue rather than the Norman or Burgundian.

The feudal system, in parcelling out the country, had
secured the independence of the chief districts in politics,
language, and literature; and similarly, when the feudal system
gave place to a central monarchy, the dialects also fell, and
were suppressed by a central language. The dialect of the
dominant province was sure to become the language of the
whole people.

Thus the language must depend on political movements;
and the election of Hugh Capet, Duke of France, to be
king, settled the question, and made Paris the capital of
France. Still, throughout the eleventh and twelfth centuries,
the Capetian sovereigns, lords of little but the Ile de France
and the Orleans territory, had no influence outside the royal
domain; and the dialects retained their independent equality.
But by the middle of the thirteenth century the sovereignty
of the Capets grew stronger, and with its growth the French
dialect also increased. The lords of the Ile de France are
always growing stronger. In A.D. 1101 they get Berry;
Picardy falls to Philip Augustus in A.D. 1203, and Touraine
after it; Normandy follows in A.D. 1204; Languedoc is
added in A.D. 1272, and Champagne in A.D. 1361.

The *French* dialect followed the triumphant progress of the
Duke of France, and drove out the dialects of the conquered
provinces. Thus, to take Picardy as an example, French
was first introduced into the official acts of the conquerors,
then into literary works, and finally it was adopted by all who
wished to be thought gentlemen. The people alone resisted
and kept their ancient speech; and the Picard, no longer
written, but only spoken by the commons, and subject to
incessant alterations, fell from the rank of a *dialect* to that

of a *patois*, that is, a spoken idiom, not recognised by the French language.

And so, in less than ' three centuries, the Norman, the Picard, and the Burgundian dialects were supplanted by that of the Ile de France, and became mere *patois*, under which attentive observation alone can discover any of the characteristics of those mediæval dialects whose monuments survive in their respective literatures.

But the final triumph of French over the neighbouring dialects was not won without a struggle, in which the victor received many a wound: a certain number of forms borrowed from the defeated dialects entered into the French language. There are words whose origin can be traced to the Norman or the Burgundian; words which are not in complete harmony with the proper analogy of the French, which are, therefore, easily recognised as strangers. Thus the hard **c** of the Latin became *ch* in the Ile de France, and *c* in Picardy: **campus, cantare, carta, castellum, campania, catus, cappa, cancellus, carricare,** &c., became in French *champ, chanter, charte, chastel, champagne, chat, chappe, chancel, charger,* &c.; but in Picardy, *camp, canter, carte, castel, campagne, cat, cappe, cancel, carguer,* &c. Now in these instances, though modern French has generally followed the *ch* form, it has not done so always; thus it has taken *campagne* in preference to *champagne*. In a few cases it has adopted both forms with different senses, though they are in reality the same word: as from **campus**, *champ* and *camp;* from **cappa**, *chappe* and *cappe;* from **cancellus**, *chancel* and *cancel;* from **carta**, *charte* and *carte;* from **capsa**, *châsse* and *caisse;* from **castellum**, *château* and *castel;* from **carricare**, *charger* and *carguer*. The same might be shewn to be true with Norman and Burgundian forms; but these may serve as a sufficient example[1].

---

[1] Such double forms as *fleurir* and *florir*, *grincer* and *grincher*,

This transformation was completed by the fourteenth century; the monarchy, previously so weak, became all-powerful, and with it rose the dialect of the Ile de France; the other dialects fell into discredit, and dropped into *patois*, while that of the Ile de France became the French language.

In brief, the popular Latin, transported into Gaul, produced at the end of eight centuries the ' Langue d'Oil,' one of whose divisions, or dialects, that of the Ile de France, supplanted all the rest, and, in the fourteenth century, became the French language[2]. The same process went on in the

---

attaquer and *attacher*, *écorcher* and *écorcer*, *laisser* and *lâcher*, *charrier* and *charroyer*, *plier* and *ployer*, are also due to the dialects, and were originally the same word. Now that the history of the language has furnished us with the true explanation, it is amusing to see the grammarians decreeing that *plier* and *ployer* are different in origin, and have all manner of distinctions between them.

[2] Let us sum up the elements of the language. Its foundation is popular Latin with a strong German element introduced in the fifth century; a few faint traces of Celtic may be noticed in it. When this language was fully formed, some oriental elements were thrown in about the thirteenth century; in the sixteenth were added a number of Italian and Spanish words; in the nineteenth several expressions of English origin were accepted; to say nothing of the scientific words drawn from the dead languages and brought in by the learned, chiefly in the sixteenth and the nineteenth centuries. The oriental elements are Hebrew and Arabic. It was a favourite theory of old etymologists that all languages are derived from Hebrew; but modern philology has proved them wrong, and has established as a law that 'the elements of language answer to the elements of races.' Now the Frenchman does not belong to the same race as the Jew; and such resemblances as may exist between their languages are accidental. When Jerome translated the Old Testament into Latin he incorporated into his version certain Hebrew words which had no Latin equivalents, as seraphim, Gehenna, pascha, &c.; from Latin they passed at a later time into French (*séraphin, géne, páque*). But they entered French from the Latin, not from the Hebrew. The same is the case with the Arabic; its relations with French have been purely accidental. To say nothing of those words which express oriental things, such as *Alcoran, bey, cadi, caravane,*

other Latin countries: the Tuscan in Italy, the Castilian in Spain, supplanted the other dialects, and the Milanais, the Venetian, the Sicilian, or the Andalusian, and the Navarrais, fell from the dignity of written dialects into the position of *patois*.

We will now study the constitution and forms of the French of the thirteenth century, and take note of the path followed by the popular Latin since the fall of the Empire, and of the distance which lies between this old French, and the French of to-day.

Every one knows that one great difference between French and Latin is that French expresses the relations of words by their *position*, Latin by their *form*,) The Latin might say equally well 'canis occidit lupum,' or 'lupum occidit canis;' but in French 'le chien tua le loup' is very different from 'le loup tua le chien.' Latin, in fact, has declensions, French has none. We ask, How has this come about? Were there always six cases in Latin? Has French never had more than one case? Let us see what answer history will give.

The tendency to simplify and reduce the number of cases appeared early in popular Latin: the rough barbarians could not grasp the more delicate shades of meaning expressed by them. They accordingly constructed a new declension to

---

derviche, firman, janissaire, &c. which were brought into the west by travellers, the French language received, in the middle ages, many Arabic words from another source: the Crusades, the scientific greatness of the Arabians, the study of oriental philosophies, much followed in France between the twelfth and fourteenth centuries, enriched the vocabulary of the language with many words belonging to the three sciences which the Arabians cultivated successfully: in astronomy it gave such words as *azimuth, nadir, zénith;* in alchemy, *alcali, alcool, alambic, alchimie, élixir, sirop;* in mathematics, *algèbre, zéro, chiffre.* But even so these words did not come directly from Arabic to French; they passed through the hands of the scientific Latin of the middle ages. In fact, the oriental languages have had little or no popular or direct influence on French.

suit their wants, far more simple, but really far less efficient,
at the cost of frequent reproduction of the same form. In
the fifth century there were only *two* cases instead of *six ;*
the nominative to mark the subject, the accusative (chosen
because of its frequent recurrence) for the object. Thenceforward the popular Latin declension was (1) subjective case,
muru-s; (2) objective case, **muru-m.** This afterwards became
the base of French declension for the first half of the middle
ages; and Old French retained these two cases in the
singular and plural. Thus Old French was originally a
half-synthetic language, half-way between synthetic Latin
and analytic modern French.

The reader is referred to the body of this book for the
vicissitudes of this declension. It disappeared in the fourteenth century: from the fifteenth century onwards the
modern form alone remained[1].

It would be a folly to regret the loss of this old declension: we can only regard it with interest as the bridge over
which the French language has passed in its journey from
the ancient to the modern world. It shews us too, once
more, how parallel in their movement have been the language and the political history of the country. In the
fourteenth century the social edifice built by mediæval feudalism begins to crumble down; after Philip the Fair comes
Charles V, who strikes a fatal blow at the independence of
nobles and clergy, and begins the reform of the monarchy,
which is carried out by Louis XI, by Richelieu, by Louis
XIV. Old French moved with the times, seeking to supply
the needs of a new form of society. The movement went on
throughout the fourteenth century; the analytical or modern
spirit rapidly gained ground: declension in two cases, varia-

---

[1] The secondary modifications, consequent on the dying out
of this declension, are considered below, pp. 89–93.

tions of dialect, were abandoned; and by the end of the century Old French was gone. The fifteenth century saw the birth of modern French. With the mishaps and the shame of the House of Valois society underwent another change; the spirit of modern times began to be felt; the Renaissance dawned. The strong and expressive language of Commines is very like modern French. , By the time of the death of Louis XI, France was reorganised, and her language nearly complete.

The opening of the sixteenth century brought in nothing new. The French of Calvin's famous 'Institution de la Religion Chrétienne' (A.D. 1535) is completely ripe and full: it expresses with ease all shades of meaning; and if the language had remained as it then was, it might have escaped the criticisms of Malherbe and the seventeenth-century savants; but it was damaged by an extravagant influx of foreign words, borrowed from Latin, Greek and Italian.

The many expeditions of Charles VIII, Louis XII, and Francis I across the Alps, made the Italian language familiar to the French. The splendour of the Italian Renaissance in literature and art dazzled the French mind, while the regency of Catharine dei Medicis gave the prestige of fashion to everything Italian. This Italian influence was omnipotent at the court of Francis I and Henry II, and the courtiers handed it down to the nation. Then appeared a number of hitherto unknown words: the old military terms *heaume, brand, haubert,* &c., disappeared, and were replaced by Italian words, as *carabine* from carabina; *gabion,* gabbione; *escadre,* scadra; *parapet,* parapetto; *fantassin,* fantaccino; *infanterie,* infanteria; *alerte,* all'erta, &c. And not only war terms: Catharine dei Medicis introduced a number of words relating to court life— *courtisan* from cortigiano; *affidé,* affidato; *charlatan,* ciarlatano; *escorte,* scorta; *cameriste,* camerista; *brave,* bravo; *carrosse,* carozza, &c. Terms of art also entered with Primaticcio and

Leonardo dei Vinci; as *balcon*, balcone; *costume*, costume; *baldaquin*, baldacchino; *cadence*, cadenza; *cartouche*, cartuccio, &c.; and lastly, commercial relations between the countries left some deposits in the language, such as *bilan*, bilancia; *agio*, aggio; *escale*, scala; *banque*, banca, &c.

The Italian party went further still, and tried to shoulder out French words in ordinary speech, and to substitute Italian ones: thus your man of taste would not deign to say *suffire, grand revenu, la première fois*, but *baster, grosse intrade, la première volte.*

To this pernicious influence may be added another, the mania for antiquity. It was a time of great classical fervour ; and the admirers of these newly disclosed treasures despised the more homely French, and wished to bring in the majesty of expression and of thought which they found among the ancients. One of them, Joachim du Bellay, ventured to set forth a celebrated manifesto entitled 'Défense et Illustration de la Langue Française' (A.D. 1548), in which he proposed a plan for the production of a more poetical and nobler language by the wholesale importation of Latin and Greek words in their natural state. He sought to ennoble the French language by borrowing largely from ancient tongues, and to enrich French poetry by introducing the literary forms employed by classical authors.

One of the Duke of Orléans' pages, Pierre de Ronsard, a gentleman of Vendôme, resolved to carry out Du Bellay's reform. He threw aside the indigenous French poetry, and abruptly introduced Latin epic poetry and Greek tragedy. Thanks to his efforts, France for two centuries regarded these two ancient forms of narrative and dramatic poetry as the only legitimate ones in point of good taste, and as alone capable of noble inspirations. Ronsard also aspired to reform the French language, and to destroy all the traditions of the past. He threw literature into a wretched course of imitation, which nearly proved fatal to its national character; he recklessly seized on Greek and Latin words, and dressed up several hundred of them with French terminations : literary Latin and Greek, which had given nothing to the French language before[1], now played their parts, and, thanks to Ronsard's school, learned words, such as *ocymore, entéléchie, oligochronien,* &c., passed in from every side. Ronsard's disciples[2] far outstripped their master. Not satisfied with creating handfulls of new words, they wished to reconstruct words already in being, and to bring the whole language nearer to the Latin type. Thus, for example, the Latin otiósus and vindicáre had produced *oiseux* and *venger;* but

---

[1] We have already shewn this for the literary Latin. As to Greek, the two languages never came in contact with one another. Marseilles, the only Greek city which could have brought this about, was at an early date absorbed by the Romans. There are indeed some few Greek words in early French, such as *chère, somme, parole;* but these do not come straight from the Greek κάρα, σάγμα, παραβολή, but through the Latin which first adopted them and handed them on.

[2] We must distinguish between the master and his school. Ronsard was very far above his followers. He had real poetical genius, and as a reformer of language many of his ideas are happy and just. He recommended the *provignement* or (graffing-in like vines) of old words, the careful study of *patois*, and the adoption from them of fresh resources for the language: he was not *tout brouillé*, as Boileau says—Boileau who treated him as his executioner rather than his judge. Let us add the verdict of M. Géruzez upon him; it is clear and true. ' Ronsard at first carried his cotemporaries by storm; and their admiration often led him astray. But he has been over-praised, and over-blackened: " c'était," as Balzac says of him, " le commencement d'un poëte." He had enthusiasm without taste. If he has failed utterly in his epic and Pindaric odes, we must not forget the true nobility of his poetry in some passages of his *Bocage Royal*, his *Hymnes*, and his *Discours sur les Misères du Temps*. M. Sainte-Beuve has shewn that in sonnets and Anacreontic pieces, Ronsard ranks very high. Malherbe, who has so happily made use of Ronsard's efforts, ought to have blamed less severely the slips of the poet who was the martyr of that cause of which he himself became the hero.'

these reformers declared such forms null and void, and ordered men to write *otieux* and *vindiquer* instead, these forms being closer copies of antiquity. This absurdity was received with boundless admiration; literature became the business of a clique, with a learned language understood only by the initiated.

At last the good sense of the nation protested against such extravagances: and Malherbe was the head of the reaction. The unnatural words, so rudely thrust in, were instantly driven out, most of these artificial creations were destroyed, and the good old French words reinstated. Still, several held their own, like *incruster* by the side of *encroûter*, *faction* and *façon*, *potion* and *poison*, &c. Malherbe may have often gone too far; but in the main he was right: he appealed from Latin and Greek to the Parisians. 'If any one asked his opinion about any French words, he always sent him to the street-porters at the Port au Foin, saying that they were his masters in language[1].'

He had scarcely done his work when a new mania attacked the language. The seventeenth century took Spain for its model. The wars of the League, and the Spanish armies in France, spread far and wide the knowledge of the Spanish language. The court of Henry IV was 'Spaniardized.' Sully tells us that the courtiers did nothing but utter Castilian cries and exclamations. Hence a number of words which now make their appearance for the first time: *capitan* from capitan; *duègne*, dueña; *guitare*, guitara; *haquenée*, hacanea; *camarade*, camarada; *nègre*, negro; *case*, casa, &c.

The Hotel de Rambouillet, the Précieuses, the Academy, and the grammarians, Vaugelas, D'Olivet, Thomas Corneille, continued the work which Malherbe had begun, but exag-

---

[1] Racan, *Vie de Malherbe.*

gerated their principle, and dried up the living sources of the language. Their task of excision and suppression was consecrated by the Dictionnaire de l'Académie (first ed. 1694), which is an alphabetical collection of all words admitted into the French language, 'par le bon usage[1].' This book is the standard of the French language, as it has existed ever since. The language underwent very little change in the eighteenth century. Voltaire made some orthographical reforms (such as *ai* for *oi*, *franç-ais* for *franç-ois*). Some grammarians (like the Abbé Dangeau) tried to introduce a phonetic spelling; others dreamt of an universal language, following the lines traced by Bacon, Descartes, and Leibnitz. 'As the philosophers were for grasping what was called "the state of nature" in man, to mark down the progress of his sentiments, passions and intelligences, so did the grammarians follow after the idea of a primitive language[2].' Philosophical grammarians (like De Brosses, Condillac, &c.) conceived that there exists some one language more natural to mankind than all others; and they strove to discover it by all means in their power.

The introduction of new terms, which seemed to be arrested after the sixteenth century, has begun again with great force in our own time. The struggle between the classicists and the romantic school, which has gone on since 1824, the growth of journalism, science and industry, and the acquaintance with foreign literatures, have all contributed to this result.

These new words are of two classes, good or bad, useful or pernicious. Under the first class come the fifteen to

---

[1] *Dict. de l'Acad. Française.* Ed. 1694. Preface.
[2] De Brosses meant by his 'primitive language,' not a supposed language whence all others were derived, but that which nature breathes into all men, as a necessary consequence of the action of the soul on the bodily organs.

twenty thousand words introduced by science and industrial necessities (*photographie, gazomètre, télégraphie,* &c.) so also those foreign words which arise from international communication. Most of these come from the English language, from politics and political economy, as *budget, jury, drawback, warrant, bill, convict,* &c.; or from sport, as *turf, jockey, festival, clown, groom, steeplechase, boxe,* &c.; or from industrial pursuits, as *drainage, tender, wagon, rail, tunnel, ballast, express, dock, stock,* &c.; to say nothing 'of naval terms[1].

By the side of these valuable novelties—valuable because they express new ideas—we have also faulty ones, expressing old ideas by new words, where older words were already in existence, and were understood by every one. In the seventeenth century every one said *fonder, toucher, tromper, émouvoir;* the nineteenth prefers *baser, impressionner, illusionner, émotionner,* &c. Journalism and the chamber have flooded us with these words, and have, besides, produced a new development of old words, by creating a number of heavy, ungraceful derivatives, as from *règle, régler,* then *réglement,* then *réglementer,* and at last *réglementation;* from *constitution, constitutionnel, constitutionnalité, inconstitutionnalité, inconstitutionellement,* &c.

It is not easy to predict the future of the French language; but it is safe to feel sure that it will owe its permanence to the balance and harmonious proportion it will establish between novelty and tradition, the necessary foundations of every language; between novelty, necessary for the expression of new ideas, and tradition, careful guardian of old ideas, and of the old words which express them.

Two lessons may be learnt from this long history of the

---

[1] It is a curious fact that many of these English words are Old French words imported into England in the eleventh century by the Normans. Thus *fashion* is the old *façon; tunnel* the O. Fr. *tonnel* (now *tonneau*); and so on.

French tongue: first, that languages are not immovable and petrified, but living, and, like all things living, full of motion. Like plants and animals they spring into life, they grow, and they decay. 'Natura nil facit per saltum;' and this is as true of language as of the rest: by slow and almost insensible change it passes, as we have seen, from the rude Latin of Roman peasants to the polished surface of Voltaire's French. And next, we learn that language, being the expression or voice of society, changes with it: the movement of the language and the people is parallel. Hence we see that no language is perfectly rigid or at rest. The critics of the eighteenth century used to speak of the French language as being *fixed* at a certain epoch, round which, in a certain narrow circle, all good examples revolve. But philology has shewn us how false it is to speak of a language as fixed; it changes with society: we may regret the style of Louis XIV, but it would be absurd to try to revive it, and apply it to our own times; the people (and after all the language is made for them) would never learn this language of a past age, for it would never be able to throw itself into the same habitual mould and manner of thought. The action of time on language, as on everything, is irreparable; we can no more restore a language to its former state than we can make the oak shrink back into its acorn. The hope of possessing perfection must indeed be renounced; it is not destined for us. 'C'est qu'en aucune chose, peut-être, il n'est donné à l'homme d'arriver au but; sa gloire est d'y marcher[1].'

---

[1] M. Guizot, *Civilisation en Europe.*

II.

THE FORMATION OF THE FRENCH LANGUAGE.

WHOEVER looks even superficially at the French language will not fail to notice a distinction between such words as *simuler, mobile, ration,* which profess to be derived closely from Latin, and other words like *sembler, meuble, raison,* coming from the same sources, but of a shorter form, and apparently farther removed from their Latin ancestry. We have seen above[1] that these are two distinct formations of words, of very different origin, though both háve come from the Latin, the one popular, the other learned; the one good, formed before the twelfth century, a spontaneous and unconscious product; the other modern, chiefly of the sixteenth century, artificial and conscious.

But this mark of difference—the greater length affected by the learned words—is an utterly exterior and superficial characteristic, with nothing certain or scientific about it. Naturalists never classify by length or size, but by internal signs and qualities; nor does philology, which is the natural history of language, distinguish popular words by their length, but by certain internal characteristics. These specific characteristics, sure touchstones by which to test popular words and to separate them from words of learned origin, are three: (1) the continuance of the tonic accent; (2) the suppression of the short vowel; (3) the loss of the middle or medial consonant.

---

[1] pp. 2-31.

CHAPTER I.

The continuance of the Latin accent.

In every polysyllabic word there is always, one syllable on which the voice rests more markedly than on the others. This incidence of the voice is called *the tonic accent,* or simply *the accent:* thus on the word *raisón* the tonic accent is on the last syllable, but in *raisonnáble* it is on the penultimate. Accordingly the *accented* or *tonic syllable* is that on which the voice rests[1]. This accent gives each word its proper character, and has been well called ' the soul of the word.' .

In French it always occupies one of two ' places : either the last syllable, in words with a masculine termination, as *chantéur, aimér, finír;* or the penultimate, when the ending is feminine, as *róide, pórche, voyáge.* Similarly the accent has one of two places in Latin : penultimate when that syllable · is long, as **cantórem, amáre, finíre;** and antepenulti-mate, when the penultimate is short, as **rígidus, pórticus, viáticum.**

Look at such words carefully, and you will see that the syllable accented in Latin continues to be so in French, or, in other words, that the accent remains where it was in Latin. This continuance of the accent is a general and

---

[1] Thus then in every word (take *bátonner* for an example) there is one accented or *tonic* syllable, and only one ; the others are unaccented or *atonic.* In *bátonnér,* the accent lies on the *e,* while the *á* and the *o* are atonic. Similarly in Latin, in **cantórem** the o is accented, the a and e are not. The reader is reminded once for all that instead of saying 'the accented syllable,' we shall speak always of the ' tonic syllable ;' and instead of 'unaccented syllable,' ' atonic ;' words which will recur over and over again. It is hardly necessary to add that this accent has no sort of connection with what are commonly called accents in French (the grave, acute, and circumflex). These are but grammatical symbols, which the reader may find considered on pp. 85, 86.

absolute law : all words belonging to popular and real French respect the Latin accent : all such words as *portíque* from pórticus, or *viatíque* from viáticum, which break this law, will be found to be of learned origin, introduced into the language at a later time by men who were ignorant of the laws which nature had imposed on the transformation from Latin to French. We may lay it down as an infallible law, that *The Latin accent continues in French in all words of popular origin ; all words which violate this law are of learned origin :* thus—

LATIN.	POPULAR WORDS.	LEARNED WORDS.
Alúmine	*alún*	*alumíne*
Ángelus	*ánge*	*angelús*
Blásphemum	*bláme*	*blasphéme*
Cáncer	*cháncre*	*cancér*
Cómputum	*cómpte*	*compút*
Débitum	*délte*	*débít*
Décima	*díme*	*décíme*
Decórum	*decór*	*decorúm*
Exámen	*essaím*	*examén*
Móbilis	*meúble*	*mobíle*
Órganum	*órgue*	*orgáne*
Pólypus	*poúlpe.*	*polýpe*
Pórticus	*pórche*	*portíque*, &c.

You will notice that the popular forms are shorter than the learned ónes; as, for example, *cómpte* than *compút*, both from cómputum. The cause is that the learned *cómput* comes from the classical Latin cómputum; the popular *cómpte* from the popular Latin cómptum.

This clearly shews the difference between classical Latin (the origin of learned French) and common Latin (parent of popular French). This fall of the penultimate atonic syllable *u* (comp[u]tum) always took place in popular Latin, as saeclum, poclum, vinclum, in the Latin comedians: inscriptions and epitaphs are full of such forms, as frígdus, vírdis, tábla, oráclum, cáldus, dígtus, stáblum, ánglus, víncre, suspéndre, móblis, póstus, &c., the French derivatives of which are obvious.

CHAPTER II.

Suppression of the Short Vowel.

We have seen that the tonic accent is a sure touchstone by which to distinguish popular from learned words. There is another means, as certain, by which to recognise the age and origin of words—the loss of the short vowel. Every Latin word, as we have said, is made up of one accented vowel, and others not accented—one *tonic* and others *atonic*. The tonic always remains; but of the atonics *the short vowel, which immediately precedes the tonic vowel, always disappears in French :* as in—

Bon(ĭ)tátem	*bonté*
San(ĭ)tátem	*santé*
Pos(ĭ)túra	*posture*
Clar(ĭ)tátem	*clarté*
Sep(tĭ)mána	*semaine* (O. Fr. *sepmaine*)
Com(ĭ)tátus	*comté*
Pop(ŭ)látus	*peuplé*, &c.

Words such as *círculer*, circuláre, which break this law and keep the short vowel, are always of learned origin; all words of popular origin lose it, as *cercler*. This will be seen from the following examples :—

LATIN.	POPULAR WORDS.	LEARNED WORDS.
Ang(ŭ)látus	anglé	angulé
Blasph(ĕ)máre	blâmer (O. Fr. blasmer)	blasphémer
Cap(ĭ)tále	cheptel	capital
Car(ĭ)tátem	cherté	charité
Circ(ŭ)láre	cercler	circuler
Com(ĭ)tátus	comté	comité
Cum(ŭ)láre	combler	cumuler
Cart(ŭ)lárium	chartrier	cartulaire
Hosp(ĭ)tále	hôtel	hôpital
Lib(ĕ)ráre	livrer	libérer
Mast(ĭ)cáre	mâcher	mastiquer
Nav(ĭ)gáre	nager	naviguer
Op(ĕ)ráre	ouvrer	opérer
Pect(ŏ)rále	poitrail	pectoral
Recup(ĕ)ráre	recouvrer	récupérer
Sep(ă)ráre	sevrer	séparer
Sim(ŭ)láre	sembler	simuler
Revind(ĭ)cáre	revenger	revendiquer,&c.

Whence an invariable rule : *The short atonic syllable, which directly precedes the tonic vowel, always disappears in French words of popular origin, but is always preserved in words of learned origin*[1].

This fact is easily explained:—learned French words come from classical Latin, popular ones from popular Latin. This short atonic syllable died out of popular Latin long before the fall of the Empire : where the classical writer had alăbáster, coagŭláre, capŭlátor, fistŭlátor, vetĕránus, tegŭlárius, popŭláres, &c., the popular dialect said, albaster,

---

[1] See my work on this subject, entitled *Du Rôle des Voyelles Latines atones dans les Langues Romanes* (Leipzig, 1866).

coaglare, caplator, fistlator, vetranus, teglarius, poplares[1], &c. Naturally, then, this short syllable found no place whatever in the French language.

CHAPTER III.

Loss of the Medial Consonant.

The third characteristic, serving to distinguish popular from learned words, is the loss of the medial consonant, i. e. of the consonant which stands between two vowels, like the **t** in matúrus. We will at once give the law of this change :—*All French words which drop the medial consonant are popular in origin, while words of learned origin retain it.* Thus the Latin **vocalis** becomes, in popular French, *voyelle,* in learned French *vocale.* There are innumerable examples of this : as—

LATIN.	POPULAR WORDS.	LEARNED WORDS.
Au(g)ústus	*août*	*auguste*
Advo(c)átus	*avoué*	*avocat*
Anti(ph)óna	*antienne*	*antiphone*
Cre(d)éntia	*créance*	*crédence*
Communi(c)áre	*communier*	*communiquer*
Confi(d)éntia	*confiance*	*confidence*
De(c)anátus	*doyenné*	*décanat*
Deli(c)átus	*délié*	*délicat*
Denu(d)átus	*dénué*	*dénudé*
Dila(t)áre	*délayer*	*dilater*
Do(t)áre	*douer*	*doter*

---

[1] These examples are all taken from an excellent work by Professor Schuchardt of Gotha, entitled *Vocalismus des Vulgär-lateins.*

LATIN.	POPULAR WORDS.	LEARNED WORDS.
Impli(c)áre	*employer*	*impliquer*
Li(g)áre	*lier*	*liguer*
Re(g)alis	*royal*	*régale*
Rene(g)átus	*renié*	*renégat*
Repli(c)áre	*replier*	*répliquer*, &c.

Thus the medial Latin consonant disappears as the word passes into French. The two vowels which were separated by this consonant then fall together : ma(t)urus becomes ma-urus. The natural consequence of this clash of fully-sounded vowels is that they are both dulled, and finally combined into one sound. Thus maturus becomes in the thirteenth century *meür*, in the sixteenth *mûr*. After the Latin t went out, the vowels of ma-urus soon get flattened into *meür*, thence they pass into a contraction of two vowels (*eü*) into one (*û*), and the circumflex accent indicates with exactness the suppression of the *e* [1].

CHAPTER IV.

Conclusion.

We have now considered the three distinctive signs which characterise popular French words;—the retention of the Latin accent, the suppression of the short atonic syllable, the loss of the medial consonant.

Popular words, by thus retaining the tonic accent in its right place, shew that they were formed from the Roman pronunciation while it yet survived; that they were formed

---

[1] This contraction, or (as grammarians style it) *synaeresis*, is studied in detail in Book I, below, pp. 80-82.

by the ear, not by the eye. But learned words, which violate the Latin accent and principles of pronunciation, are in reality barbarisms, opposed to the laws of formation of both the Latin and the French. For, long after Latin had become a dead language, they were created by the learned, who drew them out of books, and thrust them, as such, into the French language. Thus, popular words are spontaneous, natural, unconscious; learned words intentional, artificial, consciously fabricated: instinct is the mother of the former, reflection of the latter.

Hence we may understand the exact time at which the French language came into being as a historical fact. French was alive and Latin dead from the day that men no longer naturally understood the accent of the latter. This Latin accent died out about the eleventh century. The same epoch is the date of the complete creation of the French language: thenceforward none but learned words enter in. These exotics appear in great numbers in the fourteenth century; Aristotle is translated by Nicolas Oresme, Livy by Bercheure: to express ancient ideas they are compelled to fashion new words, and so they transplant from Latin into French a crowd of words without really changing their original form. Thus, Bercheure writes *consulat, tribunitien, faction, magistrat, triomphe*, &c.; and Oresme gives us *aristocratie, altération, démocratie, tyrannie, monarchie, animosité, agonie*, &c. These words violate the law of accent at every step. Bercheure writes *colonie* from colónia; Oresme *agíle* from ágilis, &c. This influx of learned words increases throughout the fifteenth century, breaks bounds and floods the sixteenth century. In the earlier part of this Introduction[1] it is shewn that this invasion, arrested by Malherbe, stood still during the seventeenth and eighteenth

---

[1] Above, p. 28.

centuries, but moved on again with renewed energy in the nineteenth.

These words, a language within a language, are more numerous than the good old words are, and many of them have already passed out of books into the common speech of men.

Now, looked at with the eyes of a philologer, a word or phrase is beautiful so far as it is regular, i. e. so far as it obeys the laws of its formation. And therefore learned words, which break the true law of accent, are vexatious blots on the surface of a language formed regularly and logically : they mar the fair arrangement and harmonious analogy of the whole. Not that we ought to erase these words from our dictionaries. 'It would be ridiculous,' says G. Paris, in his work on Latin accent, 'to try to retrace our steps : the language is a *fait accompli ;* we cannot proscribe these lawless words of learned origin ; but we may be allowed to feel regret for their introduction into the language—so much destruction have they caused to the fair frame on which it was constructed.' And consequently the language of the seventeenth century, which has fewer learned words in it than that of the nineteenth, is, in the philologer's sight, more regular, better proportioned, and therefore more beautiful than that of our own day. For the same reason, the language of the thirteenth century, which has fewer of these blemishes, seems to the philologer to be still more perfect, for its perfection springs from its obedience to law.

But this manner of valuing language can be correct only so far as we distinguish carefully between the *form* and the *expression.*

The language of the seventeenth century, so interesting to the student in literature and the artist, who examine carefully the great works it has produced, offers but little that is interesting to the philologer or the historian, who examine the language itself. In matter of *form*, if compared with the French of the previous centuries, it is a language already impoverished and overloaded with learned words : the regular structure we admired so much at the outset is altogether lost.

But considered in its *expression*, the language of the seventeenth century recovers its supremacy ; it is more analytical than that of the thirteenth century, more able to handle abstract ideas, and, as an instrument of expression, the idiom of Racine is far above that of Villehardouin.

On the other hand, in matter of *form*, the farther we go back the more the French language improves. In the twelfth century it is quite popular, with not a trace of learned words. We shall see hereafter how this regular structure, so fair at first, has been overgrown in modern French, and how false the views which would call the earlier stages of the language the barbarous ones. Thus Jacob Grimm's principle, that ' the literary period of a language is usually that of its linguistic decadence,' receives another confirmation. One might even say that instinct makes words, and reflection spoils them ; in a word, that the perfection of languages is in inverse proportion to their civilisation ; as society grows more cultivated, language becomes degraded.

Again I would remind my reader that this discussion has treated language not artistically but scientifically. Language, like the garden, may and should be studied from two points of view : the artist looks only at the beauty of the rose, the botanist studies the regularity of its structure and the place it holds in the vegetable world. So too with language ; while the literary man ought to consider it as an art, and mark its æsthetic beauty, our task is a different one : the philologer looks at *form* rather than *expression*, and seeks to discover the laws of its formation : an idiom is beautiful in his eyes when it is perfectly regular. This distinction the reader must always bear in mind. Alphabet, inflexions, formation of words—here are the three divisions into which our subject naturally falls. There is a guiding-line through this labyrinth—the strict distinction of popular from learned words; the former spontaneous and regular, the latter conscious, the arbitrary and personal work of the learned, not to be referred to any proper laws. One example will explain our meaning.

When we say (p. 60) that the Latin ct always becomes *it* in French, as *factus, fait;* octo, *huit,* &c., it is clear that we are speaking only of the popular language, and of good old words derived naturally from the 'rustic' Latin, and that we set aside such modern learned words as *traction, factum, nocturne,* &c., which are servile copies of Latin forms[1].

Thus, then, the distinction between popular and learned words forms the foundation of this book: we propose to reject every word introduced since the formation of the language. And, farther, we shall always take care to cite, when necessary, the Old French forms; for they explain the transition, and mark, like sign-posts, the road along which the Latin has passed on its way towards becoming French. We shall better see how this transit has been accomplished when the successive stages of it are under our eyes. Thus, for instance, at first sight, it is hard to see that *âme* is derived from *anima*; but history, our guiding-line, shews us that in the thirteenth century the word was written *anme,* in the eleventh *aneme,* in the tenth *anime,* which leads us straight to the Latin *anima.*

---

[1] The spelling *faict, traict,* &c., is the grotesque and barbarous work of the pedants of the fifteenth century. Middle-age French wrote, as now, *fait, trait,* &c. Wishing to make these words as like Latin as possible, the Latinists put in this *c,* without thinking that the *it* really represented already the Latin ct.

These Old French forms, natural go-betweens for the French and Latin languages, are like the runners in Lucretius who hand on from one to other the torch of life—

.   'Et, quasi cursores, vitaï lampada tradunt.'

The Latin word passes from mouth to mouth, until, in an altered shape, it reaches our own days. How can we do better, if we would find it again without hesitation, than trace it regularly through the course of its whole journey?

We are about to enter in detail on the study of these chief laws which have changed Latin into French. 'To understand the plan of the world,' says Bacon, 'we must patiently dissect nature.' By patient study of particulars we rise to laws, which are as towers up which one climbs by the ladder of experience, and from whose high top we discover a wide prospect. Strong in this great authority, we shall not be afraid of being reproached for stooping to the most minute details. The scientific mind, far from being crushed under the mass of little facts which it collects and observes, becomes stronger and more comprehensive according to the solidity with which it can found its conception of the whole on the knowledge of details. 'Wilt thou understand and enjoy the whole?' says Goethe; 'then learn to see it in its smallest parts.'

BOOK I.

PHONETICS, OR THE STUDY OF THE LETTERS OF THE ALPHABET.

PHONETICS is that part of grammar which studies the sounds of letters, their modifications and transformations. In the French language this will aim at making out the history of each of the letters transmitted to French from Latin, and will note the changes they have undergone in their transit. Thus, for example, if we take the letter *n*, we shall see that we may have, (1) permutation (that is, change), as **orphaninus** to *orphelin ;* (2) transposition, as **stagnum** to *étang;* (3) addition, as laterna to *lanierne;* (4) suppression, as infernum to *enfer*.

We have here a natural division of this study, and will consider in due order (1) the permutation, (2) the transposition, (3) the addition, and (4) the suppression, or subtraction, of letters.

In dealing with their permutations, we shall first ascend from French to Latin, and then descend in the reverse direction, from Latin to French, thus writing in due order the history of both the French and the Latin letters of the alphabet.

PART I.

PERMUTATION OF LETTERS.

CHAPTER I.

HISTORY OF THE FRENCH ALPHABET.

Imagine that each word is a living organism; then the consonants will be its skeleton, which cannot move without the help of the vowels, which are the muscles that connect the bones with one another.

Thus the vowels are the moving and fugitive parts, the consonants the stable and resisting elements of words. Consequently, the permutation of vowels is subjected to less certain laws than that of consonants; they pass more readily from one to another.

SECTION I.

ORIGIN OF THE FRENCH VOWELS.

We will consider successively the simple vowels (*a, e, i, o, u*), and the compound vowels.

§ 1. *Simple Vowels.*

Before entering on the study of vowels, let us point out to our reader the essential principle which is the key to the whole book. This is as follows: — *The popular French language keeps the Latin tonic syllable, and suppresses both the short atonic syllable and the medial consonant.*

Now every Latin word has one accented vowel and others not accented, or, in other words, one tonic and other atonic vowels. Let us examine each of these two classes separately. For example, the French *a* may come either from an accented Latin a (*arbre* from árbor), or from an atonic Latin a (*amour* from amórem).

Under each of these classes we must again distinguish (1) the vowels short by nature (schŏla), (2) those long by nature (amōrem), and (3) those long by position, i.e. those followed by two consonants (fortis)[1].

Now, in order to pursue a methodical plan, and to include every possible case, we will in each instance follow the sub-, jóined paradigm, or example of method :—

O.

This letter comes from the Latin o :

I. Either from an accented o : (1) *short,* schóla, *école;* (2) *long by nature,* pómum, *pomme;* (3) *long by position,* fórtis, *fort.*

II. Or from an atonic (unaccented) o : short, obédire, *obéir;* (2) long by nature, dōnare, *donner;* (3) long by position, conducere, *conduire*[2].

---

[1] Those long by position include, beside such words as fortis, &c., such words as peric'lum, artic'lus, pon're, contracted from perículum, artículus, pónere. Whereas the literary Latin wrote víridis, tábula, pónere, stábulum, &c., popular Latin suppressed the short penultimate (in the case of all words accented on the antepenultimate), and said vírdis, tábla, pónre, stáblum, &c., whence come the French words *vert, table, pondre, étable,* &c. This shorter form brought together two consonants (tabla); and we may class these vowels among those which are long by position. Properly speaking, we ought in all places to substitute the popular for the classical forms of Latin words; but, for fear of confusing our reader, we have not done so. But it should be remembered that, wherever such words as tábula, pónere, pósitus, &c., occur, they must be read and pronounced as táb'la, pón're, póstus, &c.

[2] To shorten matters, we will not repeat the words 'short,' 'long by nature,' 'long by position,' but will simply indicate these divisions by the figures (1), (2), (3).

A.

This letter comes from the Latin a, e, i.

I. From an elementary a :

i. Accented: (1) *chambre,* camera; *âne,* ásinus; *câge,* cávea; (2) *voyâge,* viáticum ; *sauvage,* silváticus ; *car,* quáre; (3) *flamme,* flámma; *char,* cárrus; *arbre,* árbor ; *ange,* ángelus.

ii. Atonic: (1) *salut,* salútem; *avare,* avárus; *parer,* paráre; (2) *panier,* panárium; *savon,* sapónem ; (3) *asperge,* aspáragus ; *carré,* quadrátus.

II. From an elementary e :

i. Accented : (3) *lucarne,* lucérna ; *lézard,* lacérta.

ii. Atonic : (1) *Mayenne,* Meduána ; (3) *parchemin,* pergaménum ; *marchand,* mercántem.

III. From an elementary i :

i. Accented: (3) *langue,* língua ; *sangle,* cíngulum ; *sans,* síne.

ii. Atonic : (1) *balance,* biláncem ; *calandre,* cylíndrus ; *Angoulême,* Iculísma ; (3) *sanglot,* singúltus; *Sancerre,* Sincérra ; *paresse,* pigrítia ; *sanglier,* singuláris; *sauvage* (Old French *salvage*), silváticus[1].

---

[1] The reader will remark that these Latin words are accented. I have thought this necessary, for the sake of marking clearly the Latin accent in each word.

E.

This letter comes from the Latin e, a, i.

I. From an elementary e :

i. Accented: (2) *cruel,* crudélis ; *espère,* spéro ; *règle,* régula ; *chandelle,* candéla.

ii. Atonic: (1) *légume,* legúmen ; (3) *église,* ecclésia ; *semaine* (O. Fr. *sepmaine*), septimána.

II. From an elementary a :

i. Accented. (1) *père,* páter ; *chef,* cáput ; (2) *mortel,* mortalis ; *sel,* sál ; *amer,* amárus ; *noyer,* necáre ; *aimer,* amáre ; *gré,* grátum ; *nez,* násus ; *nef,* návis ; (3) *alègre,* alácrem.

ii. Atonic: (2) *chenil,* caníle ; *parchemin,* pergaménum ; (3) *hermine,* Arménia.

III. From a primitive i :

i. Accented: (1) *trèfle,* trifolium ; (2) *sec,* siccus ; *ferme,* firmus ; *cep,* cíppus ; *mèche,* myxa ; *crête,* crísta ; (3) *Angoulême,* Iculísma.

ii. Atonic: (1) *mener,* mináre* ; *menu,* minútus ; *béton,* bitúmen ; (2) *devin,* divínus ; *deluge,* dilúvium.

IV. From a 'prosthesis,' [or addition of a letter at the beginning of a word, as *esprit,* spiritus].

I.

This letter comes from the Latin i, e, c.

I. From a primitive i :

i. Accented: (1) *sourcil,* supercílium ; (2) *ami,* amícus ; *épi,* spíca ; *épine,* spína ; *ouir,* au(d)ire.

ii. Atonic: *lier,* ligáre ; *image,* imáginem ; *ciguë,* cicúta.

E

II. From a primitive e :

i. Accented : (1) *dix*, **décem** ; *mi*, **médius** ; *hermine*,
Arménia ; (2) *cire*, **céra** ; *merci*, **mercédem** ; *tapis*, **tapétum** ;
six, **séx** ; *église*, **ecclésia** ; *Venise*, **Venétia** ; *Alise*, **Alésia** ;
(3) *ivre*, **ébrius**.

ii. Atonic : (2) *timon*, **temónem**.

III. From c :

It would be inaccurate to assert that the Latin c becomes
a French *i*, or (more generally) that any consonant becomes
a vowel ; but it has been observed that the double consonant
ct, as in **factus, tractus**, passes in French into *it, fait, trait;*
under the influence of the vowel that precedes it[1] : *trailer*,
tractare ; *fait*, **factus** ; *étroit*, **strictus** ; *toit*, **tectum** ; *biscuit*,
biscoctus ; *lait*, **lactem** ; *duit* (*reduit, conduit, produit, séduit*,
&c.), **ductus** ; *lit*, **lectum** ; *fruit*, **fructus** ; *laitue*, **lactuca** ;
voiture, **vectúra** ; *Poitiers*, **Pictávi** ; *poitrail*, **pectorále** ; *droit*,
Low Lat. **drictus**, from **directus**[2]. When the ct in the
Latin is not preceded by a vowel, the double consonant is
changed simply into *t*, as *point*, **punctum** ; *saint*, **sanctum** ;
oint, **unctum**.

O.

This letter comes from the Latin o, u, au, n.

I. From a primitive o :

i. Accented: (2) *nom*, **nómen** ; *raison*, **ratiónem** ; *pondre*,
pónere.

ii. Atonic: (1) *obéir*, **obedíre** ; *honneur*, **honórem**.

---

[1] No notice need here be taken of technical words, such as
strict (**strictus**), *réduction, induction, protection*, &c. [Such words
are found in the literary, not in the popular Latin.]

[2] The form **drictus** is frequent in Latin texts from the fifth
century downwards, and after a time entirely supplants the more
correct form **directus**.

II. From a primitive u:

i. Accented: (1) *nombre*, númerus; (2) *ponce*, púmicem; (3) *ongle*, úngula; *noces*, núptiae.

ii. Atonic: (3) *ortie*, urtíca.

III. From a primitive au:

i. Accented: *or*, aúrum; *trésor*, thesaúrus; *chose*, caúsa; *clore*, claúdere.

ii. Atonic: *oser*, ausare*; *Orléans*, Aureliáni.

IV. From a primitive n:

In a certain number of words: such as, *époux*, spónsus; *couvent*, convéntus; *Coutances*, Constántia; *moutier*, in the thirteenth century *moustier*, in the tenth *monstier*, from monastérium; *coûter* (O. Fr. *couster*), from constare.

U.

This letter comes from the Latin u, i.

I. From u:

i. Accented: (2) *nu*, núdus; *mur*, múrus; *aigu*, acútus; *menu*, minútus.

ii. Atonic: *superbe*, supérbus; *munir*, muníre.

II. More rarely from an atonic i: as *fumier*, fimárium; *buvait*, bibébat.

§ 2. *Compound Vowels.*

These are nine in number; four of them (*ai, ei, oi, ui*) formed by the help of the vowel *i*, the remaining five by the help of the vowel *u* (*au, eau, eu, ou, œu*).

AI.

This compound sound comes either from a Latin a, or from a transposition of letters :

I. From an accented a : *maigre,* mácrum ; *aile,* ála ; *caisse,* cápsa ; *aime,* ámo ; *main,* mánus ; *semaine,* septi-mána.

II. From a transposition of letters :

In this case *ai* springs from the junction of the two vowels a and i, separated in the Latin by a consonant which in the transition into French has undergone trans-position, as contrarius, *contraire*[1].

EI.

This compound sound comes from the Latin e, i.

I. From e :

i. Accented: (2) *veine,* véna ; *plein,* plénus ; *frein* frénum ; *haleine,* haléna ; *Reims,* Rémi.

ii. Atonic : (1) *seigneur,* seniórem.

II. From i : *seing,* sígnum ; *teigne,* tínea ; *sein,* sínus.

OI.

This compound vowel comes :—

I. From the reciprocal attraction of the vowels o and i separated in Latin by a consonant : *histoire,* história ; *poison* potiónem ; *temoin,* testimónium.

II. From a long e : *avoine,* avéna ; *soir,* serus ; *crois* crédo ; *toile,* téla ;- *voile,* vélum ; *hoir,* heres ; &c.

III. From i : *voie,* vía ; *soif,* sítis ; *poil,* pílus ; *poivre* píper ; *pois,* písum ; *foi,* fídes ; *poire,* pírum ; &c.

---

[1] See below, the chapter on Transposition, p. 77.

UI.

This compound vowel comes from the Latin o: *puis*, post; *cuir*, córium; *muid*, modius; *huître*, óstrea; *huis*, óstium[1]; *cuire*, cóquere; *hui*[2], hodié; *Le Puy*, Pódium. In some other cases it is the result of an attraction of the Latin vowels u and i, separated by a consonant: *juin*, junius; *aiguiser*, acutiare*.

AU, EAU.

Au is a softened form of the Latin al, eau of the Latin el.

I. From al: *autre*, alter; *aube*, alba; *sauf*, salvus; *auge*, alveus; *saut*, saltus; *jaune*, gálbinus.

II. From el: *beau*, béllus; *Meaux*, Meldi, *château*, cas-téllum.

EU, ŒU.

This compound vowel comes from an accented o: *heure*, hóra; *seul*, sólus; *leur*, illórum; *preuve*, próba; *aieul*, aviólus*; *neveu*, nepótem; *queux*, cóquus;. *feuille*, fólia; *meule*, móla; *œuf*, óvum; *cœur*, cor; *Meuse*, Mósa; *sœur*, sóror; *mœurs*, móres; *vœu*, vótum; *nœud*, nódus; *œuvre*, ópera; *couleur*, colórem; *neuf*, nóvus; *neuf*, nóvem.

OU.

This compound vowel comes from the Latin o, u, l.

I. From o:

i. Accented: *couple*, cópula; *nous*, nos; *vous*, vos; *roue*, róta.

---

[1] The Old French *huis* signifies a 'gate.' Though now obsolete, it survives in *huissier* (properly a porter, Engl. *usher*), and in the phrase 'à *huis* clos,' 'with closed doors.'

[2] *Hui* in the word *aujourd'hui*. For the explanation of this word see p. 155.

ii. Atonic: (1) *couleur*, colórem; (3) *fourmi*, formíca; *moulin*, molínum; *souloir*, soláre; *douleur*, dolórem; *couronne*, coróna.

II. From u:

i. Accented: *coupe*, cúpa; *outre*, úter; *Adour*, Atúris; *coude*, cúbitus; *four*, fúrnus; *ours*, úrsus; *tour*, túrris; *sourd*, súrdus.

ii. Atonic: *gouverner*, gubernáre; *Angoulême*, Iculísma.

III. From l:

In this case *ou* is only a softened form of the Latin ol, ul: *mou*, mollis; *cou*, collem; *écouter* (O. Fr. *escolter*), auscultáre'; *,poudre*, púlverem; *soufre*, sulphur; *pouce*, póllicem; *coupable*, culpábilis.

IE, IEU.

I. The compound vowel *ie* comes from the Latin ia, e:

i. From ia accented: *veniel*, veniális; *chrétien*, christiánus; *Amiens*, Ambiáni.

ii. From e accented: *fier*, férus; *fiel*, fél; *hier*, héri; *miel*, mél; *bien*, béne; *lièvre*, léporem; *tient*, ténet; *fièvre*, fébris; *pierre*, pétram; *rien*, rém; *hieble*, ébulum.

For the vowels *ie* in *-ier* (*premier*, primarius) see below, p. 107.

II. The compound vowel *ieu* comes from either e, as *Dieu*, Deus; or from o, as *lieu*, locus.

SECTION II.

ORIGIN OF THE FRENCH CONSONANTS.

The consonants may be divided into natural groups of Labials, Dentals, and Gutturals, answering to the different parts of the vocal mechanism.

Classification of Consonants.

LIQUIDS.	LABIALS.	GUTTURALS.	DENTALS.	
l, m, n, r.	b, v.	g, j.	d, z (s).	soft.
	p, f.	(q, k, c) ch.	t, s (x).	hard.

§ 1. Liquids: *n, m, l, r, ll, mm, nn, rr.*

N.

This letter comes from the Latin n, m, l.

I. From a primitive n :

i. Initial: *nous*, nos; *nez*, nasus.

ii. Medial: *ruine*, ruina; *règne*, regnum; *mentir*, mentiri.

iii. Final: *son*, sonus; *raison*, rationem; *étain*, stagnum.

II. From a primitive m :

i. Initial: *nappe*, mappa; *nèfle*, mespilum; *natte*, matta.

ii. Medial: *sente*, semita; *conter*, computare; *singe*, simius; *daine*, dama; *printemps*, primum-tempus.

iii. Final: *rien*, rem; *airain*, aeramen; *mon, ton, son,* meum, tuum, suum.

III. From a primitive l:

Niveau (O. Fr. *nivel*), libella[1]; *poterne* (O. Fr. *posterne*, and very O. Fr. *posterle*), posterula; *marne* (O. Fr. *marle*), **márgula.**

M.

' This letter comes from the Latin m, n, b:

I. From a primitive m:

i. Initial: *mer*, mare; *main*, manus; *mère*, mater.

ii. Medial: *froment*, frumentum; *chambre*, camera; *compter*, computáre.

iii. Final: *daim*, dama; *nom*, nomen; *faim*, fames.

II. From a primitive n: *nommer*, nominare; *charme*, cárpinùs.

III. From a primitive b: *samedi*, sabbati dies.

L. .

This letter comes from the Latin l, r, n.

I. From a primitive l:

i. Initial: *loutre*, lutra; *lettre*, littera; *langue*, lingua.

ii. Medial: *aigle*, aquila; *fils*, filius; *cercle*, circulus; *câble*, capulum.

iii. Final: *seul*, solus; *poil*, pilus; *sel*, sal; *sourcil*, supercilium.

II. From a primitive r: *autel*, altare; *crible*, cribrum; *palefroi*, paraveredus, in the fifth century parafredus; *flairer*, fragare.

III. From a primitive n: *orphelin*, orphaninus*; *Palerme*, **Panormus**; *'Roussillon*, **Ruscinonem**; *Bologne*, **Bononia**; *Château-Landon*, **Castellum-Nantonis.**

---

[1] And compare the English *level*.

R.

This letter comes from the Latin **r, l, s, n.**

I. From a primitive **r** :

i. Initial: *règne*, regnum ; *déroute*, derupta.

ii. Medial: *souris*, soricem ; *charme*, carmen ; *droit*, Low Lat. drictus for directus.

iii. Final: *ver*, vermis ; *cor*, cornu ; *enfer*, infernum ; *hiver*, hibernum.

II. From a primitive **l** :

i. Initial: *rossignol*, lusciniola*.[1]

ii. Medial: *orme*, ulmus ; *remorque*, remulcum ; *esclandre*, scándalum ; *chartre*, cártula ; *chapitre*, capitulum.

III. From a primitive **s** : *Marseille*, Massilia ; *orfraie*, ossifraga ; *varlet*, vassaletus*.

IV. From a primitive **n** : *ordre*, ordinem ; *pampre*, pampinus ; *timbre*, tympanum ; *diacre*, diaconus ; *coffre*, cophinus ; *Londres*, Londinum.

LL.

This double consonant comes from the Latin **ll, lia, lea, cl, gl, tl, chl** :

I. From **ll**: *anguille*, anguilla ; *bouillir*, bullire ; *faillir*, fallere.

II. From **lia, lea**: *fille*, filia ; *Marseille*, Massilia ; *paille*, palea.

III. From **cl, gl, tl, chl**: *oreille*, auricula ; *seille*, situla ; *veiller*, vigilare ; *treille*, trichila ; *volaille*, volatilia.

---

[1] This change of l into **r** had taken place in the late Latin texts, long before the birth of the French tongue: thus, while we find **lusciniola** in Plautus and Varro, we find in the Merovingian MSS. only the forms **rusciniola, rosciniola.**

MM.

This double consonant comes from the Latin mm, mn:

I. From **mm**: *flamme*, flamma; *somme*, summa.

II. From **mn**: *femme*, femina; *somme*, somnus; *sommeil*, somniculus*; *homme*, hominem.

NN.

This comes from the Latin mn: *colonne*, columna; or from **gn**: *connaître*, cognoscere.

RR.

This double consonant comes from the Latin tr, dr:

I. From a primitive tr: *pierre*, petra; *verre*, vitrum, *larron*, latronem; *pourrir*, putrere; *parrain*, patrinus, *marraine*, matrina.

II. From a primitive **dr**: *carré*, quadratum; *arrière*, ad-retro; *carrefour*, quadrifurcus.

§ 2. Labials: *p, b, f (ph), v, w.*

P.

From the Latin p:

i. Initial: *pain*, panis; *pré*, pratum.

ii. Medial: *couple*, cópula; *étouppe*, stuppa; *sapin* sapinus.

iii. Final: *loup*, lupus; *champ*, campus; *cep*, cippus.

B.

This letter comes from the Latin b, p, v, m.

I. From a primitive b:

i. Initial: *boire*, bibere; *bon*, bonus.

ii. Medial: *diable*, diabolus; *arbre*, arbor.

iii. Final: *plomb*, plumbum.

II. From a primitive **p** : *double*, duplus; *câble*, capulum ; *abeille*, apicula.

III. From a primitive **v** : *courber*, curvare; *brebis*, vervecem; *corbeau*, corvellus; *Besançon*, Vesontionem; *Bazas*, Vasatae.

IV. From **m** : *flambe*, flamma; *marbre*, marmor.

F, Ph.

The French language contains a great number of scientific and learned terms, like *physique*, *philosophie*, *triomphe*, in which the Greek letter φ, Lat. **ph**, is to be met with. It would be superfluous to enumerate such elementary and obvious derivations; we will therefore limit ourselves to the remark that the French *f* comes from the Latin **f**, **ph**, **v**, **p**.

I. From **f**, **ph** :

i. Initial : *faux*, falx; *faisan*, phasianus; *fumier*, fimarium.

ii. Medial : *orfraie*, ossifraga; *orfèvre*, aurifaber; *coffre*, cophinus.

iii. Final : *tuf*, tofus.

II. From a primitive **v** :

i. Initial : *fois*, vice.   (For the change of the Latin **i** into **oi**, see p. 52.)

ii. Medial : *palefroi*, parafredus, form of the common Latin for paraveredus.

iii. Final : *vif*, vivus; *suif*, sevum; *nef*, navis; *bœuf*, bovis ; *œuf*, ovum ; *sauf*, salvus ; *serf*, servus ; *cerf*, cervus.

III. From **p** : *chef*, caput; *nèfle*, mespilum ; *fresaie*, praesaga.

V.

This letter comes from the Latin **v, b, p**.

I. From a primitive **v**:

   i. Initial: *viorne*, **viburnum**; *viande*, **vivenda**[1].

   ii. Medial: *chauve*, **calvus**; *gencive*, **gengiva**.

II. From a primitive **b**: *fève*, **faba**; *cheval*, **caballus**; *avoir*, **habere**; *lèvre*, **labrum**; *souvent*, **subinde**; *ivre*, **ebrius**; *avant*, **ab-ante**; *livre*, **libra**; *niveau*, **libella**; *prouver*, **probare**; *Vervins*, **Verbinum**.

III. From a primitive **p**: *rive*, **ripa**; *sève*, **sapa**; *louve* **lupa**; *cheveu*, **capillum**; *chèvre*, **capra**; *savon*, **saponem**; *savoir*, **sapere**; *crever*, **crepare**.

§ 3. Dentals: *t, th, d, s, z, x, j.*

T.

This letter comes from the Latin **t, d**.

I. From a primitive **t**:

   i. Initial: *toison*, **tonsionem**; *taon*, **tabanus**.

   ii. Medial: *matière*, **materia**; *état*, **status**; *château*, **castellum**.

   iii. Final: *huit*, **octo**; *cuit*, **coctus**; *fait*, **factus**.

II. From a primitive **d**: *dont*, **de-unde**; *vert*, **viridis**; *souvent*, **subinde**; *Escaut*, **Scaldis**.

The Greek *th* is only found in technical and learned terms, such as *théocratie*, *théologie*, &c.

---

[1] Originally *viande* signified vegetable as well as animal nutriment. Rabelais tells us 'les poires sont *viandes* très salubres' (*Pantagruel*, iv. 54); and, so late as 1607, in his tragedy, *Le Triomphe de la Ligue*, Néréus says, speaking of God,

   ' Il donne la *viande* aux jeunes passereaux'—

a line from which Racine drew his famous

   ' Aux petits des oiseaux il donne la pâture.'

D.

This letter comes from the Latin d, t.

I. From a primitive **d** :

i. Initial: *devoir*, debere; *dans*, de-intus; *dîme*, decimus.

ii. Medial: *tiède*, tépidus; *émeraude*, smaragdus; *vendre*, vendere.

iii. Final : *sourd*, surdum ; *muid*, modius ; *froid*, frigidus.

II. From a primitive **t** :

i. Initial: *donc*, tunc

ii. Medial : *coude*, cubitus ; *Adour*, Aturis ; *Lodève*, Luteva.

iii. Final: *lézard*, lacerta ; *marchand*, mercantem.

S.

This letter comes from the Latin s, c, t.

I. From a primitive **s** :

i. Initial: *seul*, solus; *serment*, sacramentum ; *sous*, subtus.

ii. Medial : *cerise*, cerasus; *maison*, mansionem; *asperge*, asparagus; *Gascogne*, Vasconia.

iii. Final : *mais*, magis; *ours*, ursus; *épars*, sparsus ; *sous*, subtus; *moins*, minus.

II. From t followed by the compound vowels ia, ie, io, iu :

ii. Medial : *poison*, potionem ; *raison*, rationem; *oiseux*, otiosus; *Venise*, Venetia; *saison*, sationem; *trahison*, traditionem; *liaison*, ligationem.

iii. Final : *palais*, palatium; *tiers*, tertius

III. From a soft **c** :

i. Initial: *sangle*, cingulum.

ii. Medial : *plaisir*, placere ; *voisin*, vicinus ; *moisir*, mucere; *oiseau* (O. Fr. *oisel*, from the common Latin form aucellus), avicellus; *Amboise*, Ambacia.

Note that the double consonant *ss* comes from the Latin x; as for example, *essai*, exagium; *essaim*, examen; *laisser*, laxare; *essorer*, exaurare: also from an ss, as *casser*, quassare; *fosse*, fossa.

Z.

This letter comes from the Latin s or soft c.

I. From s: *chez*, casa; *nez*, nasus; *rez*, rasus (*rez-de-chaussée*); *assez*, ad-satis; *lèz*, latus; as in *Plessis-lèz-Tours Passy-lèz-Paris.*

II. From a soft c: *lézard*, lacerta; *onze*, undecim; *douze*, duodecim, &c.

X.

From the Latin x, s, c.

I. From a primitive x: *six*, sex; *soixante*, sexaginta.

II. From a primitive s: *deux*, duos; *toux*, tussis; *époux*, sponsus; *roux*, russus; *oiseux*, otiosus; *vineux*, vinosus.

III. From a primitive c: *dix*, decem; *voix*, vocem; *noix*, nucem; *paix*, pacem; *chaux*, calcem; *faux*, falcem.

J.

From the Latin j, g, i.

I. From a primitive j:

    i. Initial: *Jean*, Johannes; *jeûne*, jejunium; *jeune*, juvenis.

    ii. Medial: *parjure*, perjurium.

II. From g: *jouir*, gaudere; *jumeau*, gemellus; *jaune*, galbinus; *Anjou*, Andegavi.

III. From i: *Jérusalem*, Hierosolyma; *jour*, diurnum; *Jérôme*, Hieronymus; *goujon*, gobionem; *Dijon*, Dibionem.

For the change from i to j, see page 65.

§ 4. Gutturals: *c, q, k, ch, g, h.*

C.

C is pronounced gutturally before *a, o,* and *u,* and is then called *hard:* before *e, i,* and *œ,* it is pronounced as a dental, and is called *soft.*

I. C hard. From the hard c of the Latins, or its equivalent q:

i. Initial: *coque,* concha; *coquille,* conchylium; *car,* quare; *casser,* quassare; *coi,* quietus.

ii. Medial: *second,* secundus; *chacun* (O. Fr. *chascun*), quisque-unus.

iii. Final: *lacs,* laqueus; *onc,* unquam; *sec,* siccus.

II. C soft. From the Latin c soft: *ciment,* caementum; *ciel,* caelum; **cité,* citatem, a common Latin form much used under the Empire for civitatem.

K.

This letter is employed in French terms of mensuration, as the barbarous equivalent for the Greek χ, which ought properly to be rendered by *ch*: thus *kilomètre* is a double barbarism for *chiliomètre,* χιλιόμετρον.

Q.

This letter comes from the Latin c *hard,* qu, ch.

i. Initial: *quel,* qualis; *queue,* cauda; *queux,* coquus.

ii. Medial: *tranquille,* tranquillus; *coquille,* conchylium.

iii. Final: *cinq,* quinque.

CH.

From the Latin c *hard*[1].

  i. Initial: *chef,* caput; *chose,* causa; *chandelle,* can·
dela; *chandeleur,* candelarum [festa]; *chèvre,* capra.

  ii. Medial: *bouche,* bucca; *miche,* mica; *perche,* pertica
fourche, furca; *mouche,* musca; *secher,* siccare.

  iii. Final: *Auch,* Auscia.

G hard.

From the Latin g *hard,* c *hard,* q, v, n.

  I. From a primitive g *hard:*

  i. Initial: *goujon,* gobionem; *goût,* gustus.

  ii. Medial: *angoisse,* angustia; *sangle,* cingulum.

  iii. Final: *long,* longus; *étang,* stagnum; *poing,* pugnus

  II. From c *hard:*

  ' i. Initial: *gobelet,* cupelletum*; *gras,* crassus; *gonfler*
conflare.

  ii. Medial: *maigre,* macrum; *langouste,* locusta; *vi
guier,* vicarius; *cigogne,* ciconia.

  III. From a primitive v: *Gascogne,* Vasconia; *gui,* viscum
gué, vadum; *gaîne,* vagina; *guèpe,* vespa; *sergent,* ser
vientem; *Gard,* Vardo; *Gapençais,* Vappincensium; *gâte:
(O. Fr. gaster),* vastare; *guivre,* vipera.

  IV. From a Latin n followed by a vowel: *cigogne,* ciconia
Digne, Dinia; *Auvergne,* Arvernia; *oignon,* unionem
Boulogne, Bononia.

G soft.

From the Latin g and the suffixes ia, ea.

  I. From a primitive g:

---

[1] And from the Greek χ in such technical terms as *chirograph*
(χειρόγραφος), *chaos* (χάος), &c.

i. Initial: *gencive,* **gingiva**; *géant,* **gigantem**; *geindre,* **gemere.**

ii. Medial: *large,* **largus.**

II. From the diphthongs ia, io—ea, eo.

We learn from Quinctilian that the Roman i and j had originally the same sound. For a long time a great uncertainty existed as to the use of these two letters. Old MSS. and, after them, printed books down to the middle of the seventeenth century use *i* and *j* indifferently: it was not till the year 1750 that the French Academy recognised *j* in their Dictionary as an independent letter. This is why the Latin i in some cases has become *j* in French (or *g* soft, which is the same thing). **Hierosolyma, simia, diurnus, vindemia,** have passed into *Jérusalem, singe, jour, vendange,* proving clearly that the popular pronunciation of these words was **Hjeroso-lyma, simja, djurnus, vindemja.** This once granted, it is easy to see how **pipionem, tibia, rabies, Dibionem, diluvium, cambiare*, abbreviare,** &c., have respectively passed into *pigeon, tige, rage, Dijon, déluge, changer, abréger,* &c.[1] In these words two successive alterations have taken place: (1) from *i* into *j,* or (as the Germans call it) the 'consonni-fication' of the letter *i* (thus **pipionem** is pronounced *pipjo-nem;* **rabies,** *rabjes,* **Dibionem,** *Dibjonem,* &c.); (2) this change of *i* into *j* brings two consonants together, and into a sort of collision (**pipionem** becoming *pipjonem,* &c.). Now (as we will shew later on[2]) in such cases the first of the two consonants disappears; **subjectus** becomes *sujet,* **dorsum,** *dos;* and similarly *pipjonem, tibja, rabjes,* &c., become **pijonem, tija, rajes,** &c., whence again come *pigeon, tige, rage,* &c.

---

[1] It is hardly necessary to remind the reader that the French *j* is always a soft sibilant, not a soft mute, like our *j.*

[2] See p. 81.

Similarly, ea, eo, eu, pass into *je, ge,* &c.   In the regular Latin forms lanea, commeatus, cavea, hordeum, deusque, the e was soon replaced by *i,* and, long before Merovingian days,. inscriptions give us as the usual forms, lania, commiatus, cavia, hordium, diusque.   These diphthongs ia, iu, next exchange their *i* for *j* after the rule just noticed; and then lania, commiatus, cavia, hordium, diusque, having become lanja, comjatus, cavja, hordjum, djusque, passed naturally into *lange, congé, cage, orge, jusque,* &c.

H.

From the Latin h, f:

I. From a primitive h: *homme,* hominem; *hier,* heri; *hui* (in the word *aujourd'hui*), hodie.

II. From f: *hors,* foris; *hormis,* foris-missum[1].

CHAPTER II.

HISTORY OF THE LATIN ALPHABET.

The history of the French Alphabet has led us from effect to cause, from French to Latin; and we have ascended the stream of transformation to its source.   We must now follow the reverse course, in studying the history of the Latin letters examining and describing the modifications they have under- gone before they have descended into the French Alphabet To avoid useless repetition, we will give as few examples

---

[1] *Habler* does not come directly from the Latin, but from the Spanish *hablar* (fabulari), and cannot be traced back beyond the sixteenth century.   The Latin *f* followed by a vowel is always commuted into *h* in Spanish, if at the beginning of a word.   Thus fabulari, facere, faba, formica, become *hablar, hacer, haba hormigua.*

as possible, and will refer our readers back to the paragraphs of the first part of this subject, where he will find a sufficient number of illustrations gathered together.

SECTION I.

HISTORY OF THE LATIN VOWELS.

Every word is composed of an accented or *tonic* syllable, and of one or more *atonic*, or unaccented, syllables, which either precede or follow the *tonic* syllable. For example, in the word mercátus the a is the *tonic* vowel; e and u the *atonic* vowels. In writing the history of the Latin vowels we may study first the accented or *tonic* ones, then the unaccented or *atonic*.

§ 1. *Accented or Tonic Vowels.*

Among accented vowels we may distinguish (1) the short, (2) the long, (3) those long by position (i. e. followed by two consonants). This subdivision may seem too fine and minute; but it is in reality an important one, as will be seen by an example. Fĕrum, avēna, fĕrrum, have each an accented e, but their resultants in French are very different from one another:—the short e becomes *ie*, fĕrus, *fier;* the long becomes *oi*, avēna, *avoine;* the vowel long by position becomes simple *e*, fĕrrum, *fer.*

A. (1) ă usually becomes *ai* in French: ămo, *aime;* măcer, *maigre.* (2) ā becomes *e*: nāsus, *nez;* amāre, *aimer;* mortālis, *mortel* (3) a long by position remains *a* in French: arbor, *arbre;* carrus, *char;* carmen, *charme.*

E. (1) ĕ becomes *ie*: Iŏvium, *liége*, fĕrus, *fier.* (2) ē becomes *oi*: rēgem, *roi;* lēgem, *loi.* (3) e long by position suffers no change: terra, *terre;* lepra, *lèpre.*

I. (1) ĭ becomes *oi*: pĭrum, *poire;* pĭlus, *poil;* nĭger, *noir;* fĭdes, *foi.* (2) ī suffers no change: spīca, *épi;*

amīcus, *ami;* spīna, *épine.* (3) i long by position becomes *e* : siccus, *sec;* cippus, *cep;* crista, *crête;* firmus, *ferme.*

O. (1) ŏ becomes *eu;* nŏvem, *neuf;* mŏla, *meule;* prŏba, *preuve.* (2) ō gives also *eu* : mōbilis, *meuble;* sōlus, *seul;* hōra, *heure.* (3) o long by position remains unchanged : corpus, *corps;* fortis, *fort;* mortem, *mort;* ponere, *pondre.*

U. (1) ŭ becomes *ou* : lŭpus, *loup;* jŭgum, *joug;* cŭbo, *couver.* (2) ū remains unchanged : mūrus, *mur;* acūtus, *aigu;* pūrus, *pur.* (3) u long by position becomes *ou* : ursus, *ours;* gutta, *goutte;* surdus, *sourd;* turris, *tour*[1].

AE. ae becomes *e* or *ie* : caelum, *ciel;* laeta, *lie*[2].

AU. au becomes *o* : causa, *chose;* aurum, *or;* auricula, *oreille.*

§ 2. *Atonic Vowels.*

The tonic vowel of a Latin word always survives in French : it is not so with the atonic vowels. If we would understand what they exactly become when they pass into French, we must study (1) those which precede the tonic syllable (as the e in mercátum), and (2) those which follow it (as the u in mercátum).

(1) *Atonic Vowels which precede the Tonic Syllable.*

We may subdivide these into two classes : (*a*) atonics which *immediately* precede the tonic syllable (as the second

---

[1] Note here that short accented vowels in Latin are always represented by diphthongs in French : ă, ĕ, ĭ, ŏ, ŭ, becoming respectively *ai, ie, oi, eu, ou.*

[2] *Lie,* which in Old French signified 'joyful,' has survived in the expression 'faire chère *lie*' (literally 'to wear a glad face'), to greet one with a smiling face, give one a warm welcome, and thence to give one a good dinner, a well-known form of welcome.

i in **vindicáre**), and (*b*) those which precede it, but not immediately (as the first i in **vindicáre**).

(*a*) *Those which immediately precede the tonic syllable.* These, if long, invariably remain unchanged: **peregrínus**, *pélerin;* **coemetérium**, *cimetière;* &c. If short, they disappear[1]; **sanitátem**, *santé;* **bonitátem**, *bonté;* **christianitátem**, *chrétienté;* **positúra**, *posture;* **septimána**, *semaine;* **claritátem**, *clarté;* **comitátem**, *comté;* **clericátus**, *clergé*[2]*;* &c.

(*b*) *Those which precede the tonic syllable, but not immediately.* Short or long, these vowels are always retained in French **vestiméntum**, *vêtement;* **ornaménta**, *ornement;* &c.

(2) *Atonic Vowels which come after the Tonic Syllable.*

From the rule of Latin accentuation these vowels can only occupy one of two positions: in the penultimate (as u in **tábula**) or the ultimate syllable (as the **u** in **mercátum**).

(*a*) *In the penultimate syllable.* As this case occurs only when the word is accented on the antepenultimate (third syllable counting from the end of the word), it is always a short syllable in Latin: as **saéculum**, **lúridus**, **túmulus**, **pértica**, **pónere**, **légere**, **fácere**, &c. This vowel, being absorbed by the tonic syllable, was scarcely sounded at all, and, though the high-class Roman may have indicated it in his speech, it is certain the common people suppressed all such delicacies of pronunciation. In all the fragments of popular Latin that still remain with us (the 'Graffiti' of Pompeii, inscriptions, epitaphs, &c.) the short penultimate is

---

[1] This suppression of the short *atonic* vowel had already taken place in vulgar Latin, as we have shewn in the Introduction, p. 35.

[2] Except when they are the vowels of the first syllable of a word (as **biláncem**, **cabállus**, *balance, cheval*); for in this case the first syllable could not disappear without so mutilating the word as to destroy its identity.

gone: instead of cómpŭtum, orácŭlum, tábŭla, saéculum, pósĭtus, móbĭlis, víncĕre, suspéndĕre, &c., we find only cómptum, oráclum, tábla, saéclum, póstus, móblis, víncre, suspéndre, &c.[1] Then, when this common Latin became French, the words thus contracted became in their turn *compte, oracle, table, siècle, poste, meuble, vaincre, suspendre,* &c.

It is not necessary to say any more about this law: we may simply express it as follows:—*When a Latin word is accented on the antepenult, the penultimate vowel always disappears in the French word derived from it.*

(*b*) *In the last syllable.* This disappears in French: síccus, *sec;* cabállus, *cheval;* pórcus, *porc;* máre, *mer;* mortalis, *mortel;*—or else (which comes to the same thing) it drops into an e mute: cúpa, *coupe;* fírmus, *ferme;* &c.

SECTION II.

HISTORY OF THE LATIN CONSONANTS.

As we have seen above, consonants fall into natural groups (Labials, Dentals, and Gutturals), answering to the various parts of the vocal machinery. The permutation that goes on between Latin and French consonants rests upon two principles.

1. Permutations take place between consonants of the same class (that is, those formed by the same organ). Given, for example, the group of labials *p, b, v, f.* We know that these letters will be interchanged, but that permutation will not pass beyond their limits. Thus the Latin b becomes in French either *b* (*arbre* from arbor), or *v* as (*couver* from cubare); but it will never be permuted into, let us say, *z* or *g.*

---

[1] M. Schuchardt in his *Vokalismus des Vulgärlateins*, ii. 35, has collected a vast number of examples of this law.

2. In addition to this fact of permutation being limited to the groups, we must also notice that even within the limits of each group, permutation does not go on by chance. Thus in the labial group *p, b, v, f,* we have[1] two strong consonants, *p* and *f,* and two weak ones, *b* and *v.* All transmutation is from strong to weak. Thus the Latin b never becomes *p* in French, but the contrary transition is frequent.

We propose to refer back, as much as we can, to the examples given under the history of the French Alphabet. In addition to the simple letters we will consider also the composite ones (**lr, mr,** &c.); for they produce in French many interesting combinations.

§ 1. *Liquids :* l, m, n, r.

L.

This letter becomes in French *l, r, u.* For examples we refer the reader to these letters, above, pp. 56, 57.

tl becomes *il :* **situla,** *seille ;* **vetulus,** *vieil.*

cl, when *initial,* is unchanged in French : **clarus,** *clair.* When *final,* it becomes *il :* **oculus,** *œil ;* **apicula,** *abeille ;* **auricula,** *oreille.*

gl, when *initial,* is unchanged : **gladiolus,** *glaïeul.* When *medial,* it becomes *il :* **vigilare,** *veiller ;* **coagulare** (O. Fr. *coailler*), *cailler ;* **tegula,** *tuile.*

pl, when *initial,* is unchanged : **plorare,** *pleurer. Final,* it becomes *il :* **scopulus,** *écueil.*

bl, fl, always remain unchanged : **ebulum,** *hièble ;* **inflare,** *enfler.*

---

[1] See the tabular statement of the consonants on p. 55.

M.

In French m becomes *m, n, b.* For examples see above, pp. 55, 56, 58.

mn becomes *mm, m*: femina, *femme ;* hominem, *homme ;* nominare, *nommer ;* lamina, *lame ;* domina, *dame ;* examen, *essaim.*

mt becomes *t, nt, mt*: dormitorium, *dortoir ;* comitem, *comte ;* computare, *conter ;* semitarium, *sentier.*

N.

In French *n, r, l.* For examples see above, pp. 55–57.

nm becomes *m*: anima, *âme ;* Hieronymus, *Jérôme.*

ns becomes *s*: mansionem, *maison ;* mensem, *mois ;* insula (O. Fr. *isle*), *île ;* sponsus, *époux ;* constare (O. Fr. *couster*), *coûter.*

rn always drops the *n* at the end of words: furnum, *four ;* cornu, *cor ;* djurnum, *jour ;* hibérnum, *hiver ;* albernum, *aubour ;* carnem, *chair.*

R.

In French *r, l.* For examples see above, pp. 56, 57.

rs becomes *s*: dorsum, *dos ;* persica (O. Fr. *pesche*), *pêche ;* Lat. quercus, Low Lat. quercinus, O. Fr. *caisne, chesne,* Fr. *chêne*[1].

We must add to these changes another of no small importance, which we may call the intercalation, or insertion, of fresh letters between two liquids. Words such as humĭlis, cumŭlus, &c., whose short penultimate dropped away (see above, p. 35) became humlis, cumlus, &c. Now this com-

---

[1] Quercinus was so early corrupted into casnus that we find this latter word, used for an oak, in a Chartulary dated A.D. 508. From casnus came in the eleventh century the O. Fr. *caisne,* then *chesne,* then *chêne.*

bination of two liquids being unpleasant to the ear, the letter *b* was intercalated, and thus húmlis became *hum(b)le,* cúmlus passed into *com(b)le,* &c.

These are the intercalations:

    1. **ml** becomes *mbl*: **simulo,** *semble,* **insimul,** *ensemble.*

    2. **mr** becomes *mbr*: **numerus,** *nombre;* **camera,** *chambre;* **Cameracum,** *Cambrai,* **cucumerem,** *concombre.*

    3. **lr** becomes *ldr*: **molere** (O. Fr. *moldre*), *moudre,* **fulgur** (O Fr. *foldre*), *foudre;* **pulver** (O. Fr. *poldre*), *poudre.* The Old French forms indicate the method of the change more clearly than the modern forms do.

    4. **nl** becomes *ngl*: **spinula,** *épingle.*

    5. **nr** becomes *ndr·* **ponere,** *pondre;* **gener,** *gendre;* **tener,** *tendre;* **Portus -Veneris,** *Port-Vendres;* **veneris-dies,** *vendredi;* **minor,** *moindre.*

§ 2 *Dentals:* t, d, z, s.

T.

T becomes in French *t, d, s.* For examples see above, pp. 60, 61.

It disappears from the ends of words, whenever, in the Latin, it stands between two vowels: **gratum,** *gré;* **amatum,** *aimé;* **minutus,** *menu;* **virtutem,** *vertu;* **acútus,** *aigu;* **scutum,** *écu,* **abbatem,** *abbé.* It also disappears from the middle of words: **catena** (O. Fr. *chaéne*), *chaîne;* **maturus** (O.Fr. *maur*), *mur,* &c. This subject will be treated of more fully when we deal with the Syncopation of Consonants.

    tr becomes *r*: **fratrem,** *frère;* **matrem,** *mère;* **patrem,** *père;* **Matrona,** *Marne;* —also *rr·* **vitrum,** *verre;* **putrere,** *pourrir;* **nutritus,** *nourri;* **latronem,** *larron;* **materiamen,** *merrain;* **matriclarius** (O. Fr. *marreglier*), *marguillier.*

    st becomes sometimes (but rarely) *s*: **angustia,** *angoisse;* **testonem*** (from testa), *tesson.*

D.

In French *d, t.* For examples see above, pp. 60, 61.

dr becomes *r*: occidere, *occire;* cathedra, *chaire ;* credere, *croire;* quadragesima (O. Fr. *caraesme*), *carême.*

dj, dv drop the dental: adjuxtare*, *ajouter;* advenire, *avenir.*

nd becomes *nt*: subinde, *souvent;* pendere, *pente,* &c.

S, Z, X.

s becomes *s, c, t, z.* For examples see above, pp. 60–63.

sr becomes *tr*: crescere, *croître;* pascere, *paître;* cognoscere, *connaître;* essere*, *être* (for this verb, see Book II. Chap. I, on the Auxiliary Verbs.)

st, sp, sc, as *initials,* become *est, esp, esc*: stare, *ester;* scribere, *écrire* (O. Fr. *escrire*)*;* sperare, *espérer.* This fact is only noticed here; it will be more fully treated at pp. 78–80, in the chapter on the Addition of Letters.

x becomes *ss*: exagium*, *essai;* examen, *essaim;* laxare, *laisser;* axilla, *aisselle;* coxa, *cuisse;* exire, *issu,* past part. of *issir.*

§ 3. *Gutturals :* c, ch, gh, q, g, j, h.

C.

The soft c becomes in French *ç, s, z, x;* the hard c becomes *c, ch, g, i.* For examples see above, pp. 50, 61–64.

c between two vowels disappears, if at the end of a word: focum, *feu;* jocum, *jeu;* paucum, *peu;* Aucum, *Eu;* Saviniacum, *Savigny*[1].

---

[1] The Celtic *ak,* latinised into **acum,** indicated possession. To designate the lands of **Albinus** or **Sabinus,** the Gallo-Romans fabricated the names **Albini-acum, Sabini-acum.** This termination in the south became *ac,* in the north *ay, é,* or *y.*

cl : already treated of on p. 71.

ct : already treated of on p. 60.

Q.

See just above, under the *hard* c.

G.

g becomes in French *g, j, i.* For examples see above,
pp. 62, 64.

gm becomes *m* : pigmentum, *piment;* phlegma, *flemme.*

gn becomes *n* : malignum, *malin;* benignum, *bénin.*

gd becomes *d* : smaragda, *émeraude;* Magdalena, *Madeleine;* frigidus, *froid.*

J.

See above, p. 62.

H.

See above, p. 66.

This letter is often dropped at the beginning of words :
habere, *avoir;* homo, *on;* hora, *or;* hordeum, *orge;* hoc-illud (O. Fr. *oïl*), *oui.*

§ 4. *Labials :* p, b, f, ph, v.

P.

p becomes *p, b, v.* For examples see above, pp. 58, 59.

ps, pt, pn, as *initials.* This sound is unknown in French,
so that the p is dropped in all these cases : ptisana, *tisane;*
pneuma, *neume;* psalmus (O. Fr. *saume*). Where we find

Thus Sabiniacum is in the south of France *Savignac;* but in
the north it becomes *Savenay, Sévigné,* or *Savigny.* **Albini-acum**
similarly is *Aubignac, Aubenay, Aubigné, Aubigny.* Final *é* seems
most common in the west of France; final *y* in the centre; final
ay in Champagne and the east. But the distinction is not well-marked, and we must not lay too much stress on it.

these sounds reproduced in full *psaume, psallette,* &c., we may be sure that the words are completely modern.

pt, in the middle of words, is changed into *t, d*: **captivus,** *chétif;* **derupta,** *déroute;* **rupta,** *route;* **scriptus,** *écrit;* **adcaptare*,** *acheter;* **male-aptus**[1], *malade;* **grupta***[2], *grotte.* The words *apte, captif, crypte, rupture,* &c., are modern.

B.

b becomes *b, v.* For examples see above, pp. 58, 59.

bt, bs, bj, bm lose their *b* when they pass into French, and become *d, t, s, j, m*: **cúbitus,** *coude;* **dubitum,** *doute;* **debitum,** *dette;* **subjectum,** *sujet;* **submissum,** *soumis.*

br becomes *ur*: **abrotonum,** *aurone;* **fabrica** (O. Fr. *faurge*), *forge.*

F, Ph.

See above, p. 59.

V.

v becomes *v, f, b, g.* For examples see above, pp. 58, 59, 64.

---

[1] **Aptus** becomes in Old French *ate,* in Provençal *ade.* *Ate* or *ade* in the twelfth century bear the sense of being in good health, our 'well'; *malade,* male aptus, is one who is in bad health.

[2] **Crypta** became **crupta** in the vulgar Latin of the sixth century; and we find this word in a Latin text of the year A.D. 887 in the form of **grupta,** whence the French *grotte.*

PART II.

THE TRANSPOSITION, ADDITION, AND SUBTRACTION OF LETTERS.

CHAPTER I.

OF TRANSPOSITION (OR METATHESIS.)

When the letters of a derivative are arranged in an order different from that which they held in the word from which it is derived, we say that it has suffered *metathesis* (μετάθεσις), that is to say, transposition; as when the gn of the Latin stagnum becomes *ng* in the French derivative *étang*.

SECTION I.

TRANSPOSITION OF CONSONANTS.

N : *étang*, stagnum ; *poing*, pugnus ; *teignant*, tingentem.
L : *Lot*, Oltis.

R : *pour*, pro ; *trcuil*, torculus ; *pauvreté*, paupertatem ; *truffe*, tuber ; *troubler*, turbulare* ; *Durance*, Druentia ; *brebis*, vervecem ; *tremper*, temperare ; *fromage*, *formaticum ; *trombe*, turbo.

SECTION II.

TRANSPOSITION OF VOWELS.

The vowel *i* is often drawn towards the vowel which precedes it, whence results a necessary transposition : *gloire*, gloria ; *histoire*, historia ; *memoire*, memoria ; *juin*, junius ; *muid*, modius ; *faisan*, phasianus.

CHAPTER II.

OF THE ADDITION OF LETTERS. `

The letters added to the primitive word may be either
(1) *prosthetic* (πρόσθεσις), that is to say, put at the beginning
of a word; (2) *epenthetic* (ἐπένθεσις), or put in the body of a
word; or (3) *epithetic* (ἐπίθεσις), or put at the end of a word[1].

SECTION I.

ADDITION AT THE BEGINNING OF A WORD (PROSTHESIS).

§ 1. *Vowels.*

Before the initial sounds *sc, sm, sp, st* (which are hard to
pronounce), the French have placed an *e*, which renders
the sound more easy by doubling the *s*: *espace*, **spatium**
espèce, **species**; *espérer*, **sperare**; *estomac*, **stomachum**
esclandre, **scandalum**; *esprit*, **spiritus**; *ester*, **stare**; *escabeau*
scabellum; *escient*, **scientem**; *esclave*, **slavus***; *escalier*
scalarium[2]. After the sixteenth century several of these
words undergo a farther modification: the *s* goes out, and
its suppression is marked by the acute accent, which is
placed upon the initial *é*: *état*, **statum**; *épice*, **species**; *échelle*
scala; *écrin*, **scrinium**; *étain*, **stannum**; *étable*, **stabulum**
étude, **studium**; *épais*, **spissus**; *école*, **schola**; *étroit*, **strictus**

---

[1] These technical names, borrowed from the Greek gram
marians, are here preserved, because they are in use, and are
convenient in point of brevity.

[2] As has often been said, the French language springs not
from the literary Roman tongue, but from the popular or vulgar
Latin. Now, in the fifth and sixth centuries, the vulgar Latin
had ceased to say **spatium, sperare, stare**, &c., but **ispatium
isperare, istare**, as one sees by the inscriptions and diploma
of the Merovingian period. This i, thus prefixed by the people
to facilitate the emission of these sounds, becomes *e* in French
ispatium, *espace*; **istare**, *ester*; **isperare**, *espérer*; &c.

époux, sponsus ; *épine,* spina ; *épi,* spica , *étoile,* stella ; *épée,* spatha ; *Écosse,* Scotia[1].

By a false assimilation an *e* has been also prefixed to a number of words which, in the Latin, had no *s* : *écorce,* corticem ; *escarboucle,* carbunculus, &c.

§ 2. *Consonants.*

1. *h* added : *huit,* octo ; *huile,* oleum ; *haut,* altus ; *huître,* ostrea ; *hièble,* ebulum ; *hache,* ascia ; *huis*[2], ostium ; *hurler,* ullare (vulgar Latin form of ulŭlare).

2. *g* added : *grenouille*[3], ranuncula.

3. *t* added : *tante* (O. Fr. *ante*[4]), amita.

4. *l* added (by the junction of the article with the word) : *Lille,* illa-insula ; *lierre,* hedera ; *luette,* uvetta ; *lors,* hora ; *lendemain,* O. Fr. *l'endemain*[5].

SECTION II.

ADDITIONS IN THE BODY OF THE WORD (EPENTHESIS).

1. *h* added : *Cahors,* Cadurci ; *envahir,* invadere ; *trahir,* tradere ; *trahison,* traditionem.   The middle ages, here falling in with both the etymology and the historic reason of the words, wrote more logically *envaïr, traïr, traïson.*

2. *m* added : *lambruche,* labrusca.

3. *n* added : *langouste,* locusta ; *lanterne,* laterna ; *Angoulême,* Iculisma ; *convoîter,* cupitare* ; *concombre,* cucumerem ; *jongleur,* joculatorem ; *peintre,* pictorem.

---

[1] We pass over technical terms, like *scandale, stomacal, stoïque,* &c.

[2] For *huis* and its derivative *huissier,* see p. 53.

[3] *Grenouille* in Old French is *renouille,* a form which does not come from the classical ranúncula, but from the vulgar Latin ranúcla, a word which is often met with in MSS. of the sixth century.   On the change of *cl* into *il* (ranucla, *renouille*), see above, p. 71.   [4] Cp. the English *aunt.*

[5] Instead of saying *le lendemain, le lierre, la luette,* which are gross errors of the fifteenth century, the more correct forms *l'endemain, l'ierre, l'uette,* were in use throughout the middle ages.

4. *r* added: *fronde*, funda; *perdrix*, perdicem; *trésor* thesaurus.

5. For the addition of a *b* between the liquids *mr*, *ml* &c. (as *chambre*, camera, &c.), see above, p. 72.

SECTION III.

ADDITION AT THE END OF A WORD (EPITHESIS).

s added: *lis*, lilium; *legs*, legatum; *tandis*, tam diu; *jadis* jam diu; *sans*, sine; *certes*, certe, &c.

CHAPTER III.

OF THE SUBTRACTION, OR DROPPING, OF LETTERS

Letters withdrawn from the primitive words may be taken from (1) the beginning of the word (*aphaeresis*, ἀφαίρεσις) or (2) from the body of the word (*syncope*, συγκοπή); o (3) from the end (*apocope*, ἀποκοπή).

SECTION I.

OMISSION FROM THE BEGINNING OF THE WORD (APHAERESIS)

§ 1. *Of Vowels.*

Boutique, apótheca; *blé*, ablatum; *migraine*, ἡμικρανία *leur*, illorum; *riz*, oryza; *diamant*, adamantem; *le*, ille *Gers*, Egirius; *sciatique*, ischiadicus; *Natolie*, Anatolia.

§ 2. *Of Consonants.*

Tisane, ptisana; *pâmer*, spasmare*; *loir*, gliris; *neum* pneuma; *or*, hora; *orge*, hordeum; *on*, homo; *avoir*, habere

SECTION II.

OMISSION FROM THE BODY OF THE WORD (SYNCOPE).

§ 1. *Syncope of Vowels.*

We have seen (above, pp. 67, 68) under what law the Latin vowels passed into the French language: the *tonic* vowe always remained, but the *atonic* vowels varied; if short, they disappeared in two positions, (1) from immediately before the tonic vowel, as posĭtúra, *posture;* and (2) when they are penultimate, as regŭla, *règle;* but, if long, the atonic vowel always remained.

§ 2. *Syncope of Consonants.*

In every word the consonants can occupy two positions which differ with regard to the vowels: either (1) they are put between two vowels, as the b in tabanus, in which case they are called 'medial;' or (2) they are followed by another consonant, as b in submissum, when they are called 'non-medial.'

1. *Non-medial Consonants.* In the case of two consonants together, like bm in submissum, the former usually disappears in the French derivative: *sujet,* subjectum; *soumis,* submissus; *deroute,* derupta; *noces,* nuptiae; *chétif,* captivus; *peser,* pensare; *avoué,* advocatus; *coquille,* conchylium[1], &c. Thus too the Latin s which had survived in most French words up to the end of the sixteenth century (cp. the O.Fr. *aspre, pastre, paste,* from the Lat. asper, pastor, pasta*), disappeared in the seventeenth century, and its suppression was denoted by the introduction of a circumflex accent: *âpre, pâtre, pâte*[2].

2. *Medial consonants.* The dropping-out of these is an important element in the formation of the French language.

(1) Dentals, d: *cruel,* crudelis; *suer,* sudare; *dénué,* denudatus; *moelle,* medulla; *obéir,* obedire.

---

[1] The subject of the syncope of consonants has hitherto been but little studied, and it is not yet known what exact law it follows.

[2] Except in the case of the three words *mouche,* musca; *louche,* luscus; *citerne,* cisterna, in which the s disappeared much earlier.

t: *douer*, dotare; *muer*, mutare; *rond*, rotundus; *saluer* salutare.

(2) Gutturals, c: *plier*, plicare; *jouer*, jocare; *voyelle* vocalis; *délié*, delicatus; *prier*, precari.

g: *nier*, negare; *géant*, gigantem; *nielle*, nigella; *aoû* augustus; *maître*, magister.

(3) Labials, b: *taon*, tabanus; *viorne*, viburnum *ayant*, habentem.

v: *paon*, pavonem; *peur*, pavorem; *viande*, vivenda[1] *aïeul*, aviolus*.

SECTION III.

CONSONANTS DROPPED AT THE END OF THE WORD (APOCOPE

§ 1. *Apocope of Vowels.*

On this subject see above, p. 70.

§ 2. *Apocope of Consonants.*

t: *gré*, gratum; *aimé*, amatus; *aigu*, acutus; *éc* scutum; *abbé*, abbatem; &c.

n: *four*, furnus; *chair*, carnem; *cor*, cornu; *hive* hibernum; *jour*, diurnum; *cahier* (O. Fr. *quaier*), quate num; *aubour*, alburnum.

l: *oui* (O. Fr. *oïl*), ho[c]-illud; *nenni* (O. Fr. *nennil* non-illud.

---

[1] See above, p. 33.

PART III.

PROSODY.

Prosody is that part of grammar which treats of the modifications of vowels arising from quantity and accent. Vowels can be modified in three ways. (1) In their *nature:* e.g. *a* may become *o*. The study of these modifications will be found under the head of the Permutation of Vowels on pp. 48–54. (2) In their *length:* they may be short, as in *patte*, or long as in *pâtre*. Here we have the study of quantity. There is but little to be said about it, except that it is very vague in the French language; it is never certain except in such words as *mûr* (O. Fr. *meür*, Lat. *maturus*), which words are contractions; or in such words as *pâtre* (O. Fr. *pastre*), in which the *s* has been dropped. In these two sets of words the vowel is certainly long. (3) In their elevation or accentuation. They may be *tonic*, as the *a* in *célibat*, or *atonic*, as the *a* in *pardon*. This is the study of accent. Now there are four kinds of accent, which must be kept distinct, though they are often confounded together :—Tonic, Grammatical, Oratorical, and Provincial.

I. *Tonic Accent.*

In the Introduction we described 'tonic accent,' or more simply 'accent,' as the incidence of the voice upon one of the syllables of a word. Thus in the word *raisón*, the tonic accent lies on the last syllable, but in *raisonnáble* it is on the penultimate.

The accented or tonic syllable is, therefore, that or which more stress is laid than on any of the others. In Greek this elevation of the voice is called τόνος or προσῳδία words rendered in Latin by *accentus.*

This tonic accent gives to each word its special character and has been rightly called 'the soul of the word.' In French the tonic accent always occupies one of two places: either (1) it is on the last vowel, when the termination is masculine as *chanteúr, aimér, finír, seigneúr;* or (2) ôn the last vowel bu one, when the termination is feminine, as *sauvóge, vérre, pórch.* In Latin also the accent occupies one of two places: the penultimate, when that syllable is long, as **cantórem, amáre finíre, seniórem;** or the antepenult, when the penultimate syllable is short, as **sylváticus, pórticus.** If the reader wil compare these French and Latin examples, he will notice at once that the Latin accent survives in the French; tha is to say, the accented syllable in Latin is also the accented syllable in French (**cantórem,** *chanteúr;* **amáre,** *aimér,* **finíre,** *finír;* **seniórem,** *seigneúr.*

This continuance of the Latin accent is a matter of con siderable importance, and is, we may fairly say, the key to the formation of the French language. Its importance ha been explained in the Introduction, to which (pp. 32–35 the reader is now referred.

II. *Grammatical Accent.*

In French grammar there are three accents – acute, grave circumflex. Accent, in this sense, is a grammatical sign which has three different functions in orthography.

(1) Sometimes the accent indicates what is the proper pro nunciation of certain vowels, as *bonté, règle, pôle.* (2) Some times it marks the suppression of certain letters, as *pâtre* pastor; *âpre,* asper; *âne,* asinus; which words in Old French were *pastre, aspre, asne.* (3) And lastly it is used

to distinguish between words otherwise spelt alike, but of different significations; as, *du* and *dû, des* and *dès, la* and *là, tu* and *tû, sur* and *sûr,* &c.[1]

III. *Oratorical Accent.*

The tonic accent affects syllables within words, but oratorical accent (otherwise styled 'phraseological') influences words within sentences.　Thus oratorical accent belongs to the domain of declamation and rhetoric, and naturally has had no influence on the transformation of Latin into French words[2].　We shall therefore have no need to trouble ourselves with it in this place.

IV. *Provincial Accent.*

By provincial accent we understand the intonation peculiar to each province, differing from the intonation of good Parisian pronunciation, which is taken as the standard.　And this is in reality what is meant by the phrase, 'He who speaks French well has no accent'—that is, no provincial accent.　The study of these characteristics of the inhabitants of certain districts does not belong to our subject, and is therefore set aside.　Let us, however, say that provincial pronunciation limits itself to this—it gives a word two accents, and lowers the value of the principal (or proper) one by subjoining to it a slight half-accent on another syllable.

---

[1] Cp. Littré, *Dict. Hist.* s. v. 'Accent.'　These French grammatical accents which act as signs in writing differ widely from those of the Greek language, though borrowed from them.　The acute, grave and circumflex accents in Greek simply denote the tonic syllable, and the shades of intonation on that syllable.　In French, on the contrary, these accents have no connection with the tonic and etymological accent, and are purely orthographic symbols.

[2] See G. Paris, *Accent latin,* p. 8.

BOOK II.

INFLEXION, OR THE STUDY OF GRAMMATICAL FORMS.

BOOK II will be entirely given up to the study of inflexions; that is to say, of the modifications undergone by a noun when declined, by a verb when conjugated. Declension, of substantive, article, adjective, and pronoun, and conjugation of verbs, will naturally form the two divisions of this Book.

To make the study of the different parts of our subject complete, we will under this division include all invariable, as well as inflected, words.

PART I.

DECLENSIONS.

CHAPTER I.

THE SUBSTANTIVE.

Let us take in order (1) case, (2) number, and (3) gender.

SECTION I.

CASE.

Of the six cases of Latin declension, the nominative alone indicated the subject, the other five the 'government' or relation.

Now if we place Latin and French side by side we shall see that the six cases of the mother tongue are reduced to one in the daughter language. How has this come about? Have those six cases always existed in Latin, or has the French never had more than one? We must again turn to the history of the language; it will provide us with an answer.

The tendency to <u>simplify</u> and reduce the number of cases was early felt in the popular Latin: the cases expressed shades of thought too delicate and subtle for the coarse mind of the Barbarian. And so, being unable to handle the learned and complicated machinery of the Latin declensions, he constructed a system of his own, simplifying its springs, and reducing the number of the effects at the price of frequently reproducing the same form. Thus the Roman distinguished by means of case-terminations the place where one is, from the place to which one is going: 'veniunt ad domum,' 'sunt in domo.' But the Barbarian, unable to grasp these finer shades, saw no use in this distinction, and said, in either case alike, 'sum in domum,' 'venio ad domum.'

Thus, from the fifth century downwards, long before the first written records of the French language, popular Latin reduced the number of cases to two: (1) the nominative to mark the subject; and (2) that case which occurred most frequently in conversation[1], the accusative, to mark the object or relation. From that time onwards the Latin declension was reduced to this:—subject, muru-s; object, muru-m.

The French language is the product of the slow development of popular Latin; and French grammar, which was originally nothing but a continuation of the Latin grammar, inherited, and in fact possessed from its infancy, a completely regular declension: subject, *mur-s* muru-s; object, *mur*, muru-m: and people said 'ce *murs* est haut'; 'j'ai construit un *mur*[2].'

This declension in two cases forms the exact difference between ancient and modern French. It disappeared in the fourteenth century (as we will explain later on), not without leaving many traces in the language, which look like so many insoluble exceptions, but find their explanation and

---

[1] The fact (which had previously been pointed out by Raynouard) was completely established by M. Paul Meyer in 1860, in an Essay before the 'School of Chartularies,' with proofs drawn from the study of Latin MSS. of the Merovingian era.

[2] One can see at a glance the consequence of this distinction of cases; so long as the sense of a word is given by its form (as in Latin) and not by its position (as in Modern French), inversions are possible. Consequently they are frequent in Old French. One could say equally well, 'le *rois* conduit le cheval;' or, as in Latin, 'le cheval conduit le *rois* (caball*um* conducit re*x*).' The *s* which marked the subject (*rois*, *rex*), made ambiguity impossible.

historic justification in our knowledge of the Old French declension.

This takes three forms, answering to the three Latin declensions :—

I.

Sing. { Subjective   **rósa** .. .. .. *rose*
      { Objective   **rósa-*m*** .. .. *rose*

Plur. { Subjective   **rósae**   .. .. *roses*
      { Objective   **rósa-*s*** .. ... *roses*

2.

Sing. { Subjective   **múru-*s*** .. .. *murs*
      { Objective   **múru-*m*** .. .. *mur*

Plur. { Subjective   **múr-*i*** .. .. *mur*
      { Objective   **múr-*os*** .. .. *murs*

3,

Sing. { Subjective   **pástor** .. .. *pâtre (pastre[1])*
      { Objective   **pastór-*em*** *pasteur.*

Plur. { Subjective   **pastór-*es*** .. *pasteurs*
      { Objective   **pastór-*es*** .. *pasteurs.*

In the subjective it ran thus : ' la *rose* est belle ;' ' le *mur* est haut ;' ' le *pâtre* est venu ;' in the objective, ' j'ai vu la *rose*, le *mur*, le *pasteur*,' &c.[2]

On looking into these declensions one is struck with the facts that (1) the Latin accent is always respected ; and

---

[1] *Pâtre*, in Old French *pastre*. *Pastre* and *pasteur* were not in Old French two distinct words, but only the two cases of the same word.

[2] In all these examples of Old French, we ought to have written *li murs*, not *le murs*, *li* being the nominative singular, and *le* the accusative (as may be seen below, p. 100, in the chapter on the Article) : but as we wish to pass gradually from the known to the unknown, we have for the moment sacrificed correctness to convenience.

(2) that (with the exception of one case) the Old French takes *s* whenever the Latin has it: in other words, the French declension rests on the natural laws of derivation.

Between Latin, a synthetic language, and Modern French, which is analytic, there is an intermediate, or half-synthetic, period. This transition period is marked by the Old French declension, which indicates a resting-point between synthesis and analysis[1]. But this system was still too complicated for the minds of men in the thirteenth century: though the Barbarians had reduced the six Latin cases to two, it was conceived that it would be far more regular to reduce the three French declensions to one. Accordingly, the second declension was taken as the common form, as it was the most generally used, and its laws were applied to both the others. Now the characteristic of this second declension was an *s* in the subjective case of the singular—'murs,' murus, and accordingly, in violation of the genius of the language and of the laws of Latin derivation, men took to saying 'le pastres,' as they were wont to say 'le murs.' The laws of derivation were broken, because the Latin pástor has no *s* in the nominative; nor has it any need of that letter, since it is itself distinguished from the

---

[1] Raynouard, who in A.D. 1811 developed the laws of French declension, gave them the general name of 'the rule of the *s*,' by reason of the *s* which so commonly marks the subject. This discovery is one of the greatest services ever rendered to the study of Old French, and to the history of the language. 'Without this key,' Littré says most truly, 'everything seemed to be an exception or a barbarism; with it there is brought to light a system, far shorter indeed than the Latin, but still neat and regular.' Much discussion has taken place as to the usefulness and exact application of this 'rule of the *s*' during the middle ages: its practical utility is doubtless restricted, and it has often been broken through; but the existence of the rule (even more than its utility) is a fact of extreme interest, as it allows us to mark the stages of transition from Latin to French, and is, as it were, a halt in the passage from synthesis to analysis.

accusative **pastórem** by the position of the tonic accent
This addition of an *s* to the nominative of all such words as
pástor, which has two forms in French (*pastre, pasteur*
seemed to simplify the inflexion of nouns; but in reality
complicated it, and has in fact destroyed the whole system
of French declension.   For hereby the French declension
which had previously rested on the natural laws of deriva
tion, came to be founded on this suffix *s*, which is nothing
but an arbitrary and artificial form.   In its first period (nintl
to twelfth century) this declension depended on etymology
in its second (twelfth to fourteenth century) it rested on
mere analogy: the former is natural, the latter artificial; the
former came from the ear, the latter from the eye.

Thus then, in its first epoch, the declension was, as we
have just seen, natural, based on etymology and the laws o
derivation; but for that very reason it was specially fragile
' since its rules were only second-hand,—in other words, i
had relations with Latin forms and accentuation, but had
no stability or guarantee in the proper junction and knitting
together of its own tongue [1].'   And so French declension
was destined to perish forthwith, and the unlucky reform
which consisted in combining the three declensions in one
by sacrificing the rarer and more individual forms to the
more general ones, did not save it from ruin.   Rejected
from the speech of the populace, from the thirteenth cen
tury downwards, and constantly violated even by the learned
French declension was thoroughly ruined by the time i
reached the fourteenth century.   It disappeared, and the dis
tinction between the subjective and objective cases perished
thenceforward one case alone was used for each number
And this was the objective (or accusative) case (**falcónem**
faucon) ; for it was usually longer and more consisten

---

[1] M. Littré.

than the subjective (or nominative), and occurred more frequently in course of conversation. Thenceforth the subjective case vanished (falco, O. Fr. *fauc*), and modern declension was established

This adoption of the objective case, as the type and form of the Latin substantive had a curious result in the formation of the numbers. In the older declension we had—

	SINGULAR.		PLURAL.	
Subject	murus	*murs*	muri	*mur*
Object	murum	*mur*	muros	*murs*

where the objective case was in the sing *mur*, in the plur. *murs*. In the fourteenth century the new declension took, as we have said, the objective for its type, and consequently the *s* of the older objective case *murs* (muros), became the mark of the plural, while the absence of *s* for the objective sing. *mur* (murum) became the mark of the singular. But had the subjective case been taken as the type, and the objective abandoned, instead of the contrary, we should have had *murs* (murus) in the singular, and *mur* (muri) in the plural, so that the *s*, which now marks the plural in that case, would have distinguished the singular instead.

From the moment that final *s* ceased to be the characteristic of the cases, and became the distinctive mark of the numbers, the French mediæval system of declensions ceased to exist; the fifteenth century utterly ignored it; and when, in the time of Louis XI, Villon attempted to imitate in a ballad the language of the thirteenth century, he failed to observe the 'rule of *s*,' and his imitation consequently wants the distinctive mark of the middle ages   It is curious to see in the nineteenth century the detection of the mistakes committed by a writer who in the fifteenth tried to write a ballad in the manner of the thirteenth.

Since declension in two cases was, as we have seen, the distinctive and fundamental characteristic of Old French, the loss of these cases immediately established between Old and Modern French a line of demarcation far more distinct than any which exists in Italy or Spain between the language of the thirteenth and that of the nineteenth centuries.

There survived, however, some important traces of the Old French declension, which look to us like inexplicable anomalies—explicable, in truth, only by a knowledge of the history of the language. Before entering on the study of gender let us re-state the consideration of the Old French declensions one by one, and so discover the traces they have left in modern French.

1. *Second Declension.* Here we have suppressed the subjective, retained the objective case (*mur* from murum, *serf* from servum, &c.). Still, some relics of the subjective case are retained in the nine following words: *fils*, filius; *fonds*, fundus; *lacs*, laqueus; *legs*, legatus; *lis*, lilius; *lez*, latus[1]; *puits*, puteus; *rets*, retis; *queux*, coquus. In Old French these words all had also the objective case— *fil*, filium; *fond*, fundum; *lac*, laqueum; *leg*, legatum; *li*, lilium; *lé*, latum; *puit*, puteum; *ret*, retem; *queu*, coquum. In these instances, then, the objective case has disappeared, while the subjective has survived[2].

In this way we may explain by the history of the second declension the formation of the plural in *aux*: *mal, maux ; cheval, chevaux,* &c.

---

[1] *s, x, z,* regarded as orthographic signs, are equivalents in Old French; *voix* was written indifferently *voix, vois,* or *voiz.* A trace of this usage remains in *nez,* nasus; *lez,* latus; and in those plurals which end in *x* (*cailloux, feux, maux*), which used in Old French to be written with either an *s* or an *x*.

[2] It is just the same in the case of certain proper names, *Charles,* Carolus; *Louis,* Lodovicus; *Vervins,* Verbinus; *Orléans,* Aurelianus; &c.

In the thirteenth century the second declension was as follows :—

SINGULAR.		PLURAL.	
mals	malus	*mal*	mali
mal	malum	*mals*	malos

But the *l* is softened into *u* when it is followed by a consonant (as *paume,* palma ; *aube,* alba ; *sauf,* salvus), and so *mals* became *maus.*

SINGULAR.		PLURAL.	
maus	malus	*mal*	mali
mal	malum	*maus*	malos

Thus, when the fourteenth century abolished declension by abandoning the subjective case, and keeping only the objective, they had only *mal* (malum) in the singular, and *maus* or *maux* (malos) in the plural. So too *chevaux, travaux,* &c., may be traced.

2. *Third Declension.* In this declension in Latin the accent is displaced in the oblique cases (pástor, pastórem) ; whence it follows, as we have seen, that the third French declension had a double form: the one *pastre* (pástor) in the subjective case ; the other *pasteur* (pastórem) for the objective. In this declension, as in the second, the objective case got the mastery at the same epoch, as may be seen by looking at a few instances :—

SUBJECTIVE.		OBJECTIVE.	
ábbas	*abbe*	abbátem	*abbé au*
fálco	*fauc*	falcónem	*faucon*
látro	*lerre*	latrónem	*larron*
sérpens	*serpe*	serpéntem	*serpent*
ínfans	*enfe*	infántem	*enfant*

Here the subjective cases have all perished, the objective cases have survived.

There are a very few instances to the contrary, in which the subjective case has been retained :—

SUBJECTIVE.		OBJECTIVE.	
sóror	*sœur*	sorórem	*seror*
píctor	*peintre*	pictórem	*painteur*
antecéssor	*ancêtre*	antecessòrem	*ancesseur*
tráditor	*traître* (O.Fr.*traître*)	traditórem	*traiteur*

In many other words the two forms have survived side by side; but instead of continuing to be the two cases of one word, they have become two different words: as—

cántor	*chantre*	cantórem	*chanteur*
sénior	*sire* (O.Fr. *sinre*)	seniórem	*seigneur*[1]

SECTION II.

GENDERS.

The French language has adopted only the masculine and feminine genders, rejecting the third Latin gender, the neuter. The student of grammar must approve of this suppression of the neuter, for the Latin tongue had utterly lost all appreciation of the reasons which had originally made this or that object neuter rather than masculine; and furthermore Low Latin, by uniting these two genders in one, had prepared the way for this simplication of language, which was afterwards adopted in the Romance languages. The neuter is useless except when, as in the case of English, it belongs exclusively to whatsoever is neither male nor female.

---

[1] The Latin genitive left some traces in Old French. It is vain to quote these forms, as Modern French has rejected them all with the exception of *leur*, illorum, and *chandeleur*, candelarum (festa).

This suppression of the neuter, which dates very far back,
—long, indeed, before the irruptions of the Barbarians,—
was brought about in two ways :—

1. Neuter substantives were altered to masculines. Even
in Plautus we find **dorsus, aevus, collus, gutturem, cubitus,**
&c. : in inscriptions dating back beyond the fourth century,
we have **brachius, monumentus, collegius, fatus, metallus,**
&c. : in the Salic law, **animalem, retem, membrus, ves-**
tigius, precius, folius, palatius, templus, tectus, stabulus,
judicius, placitus, &c. It is useless to multiply proofs of
this fact, which a rhetorician of the Empire, Curius Fortu-
natianus, who flourished about A.D. 450, had already observed, and transmitted to posterity in these words, 'Romani
vernacula plurima et neutra multa masculino genere potius
enunciant, ut *hunc* theatrum, et *hunc* prodigium[1].'

2. Neuter substantives became feminines, the neuter
plural in a (**pecora**) having been mistaken (a strange error!)
for a singular nominative of the first declension. In texts of
the fifth century we find such accusatives as **pecoras, per-**
gamenam, vestimentas, &c.

We may now notice certain peculiar points which will
help us to explain such anomalies as *amour, orgue, hymne,*
délices, which are true grammatical irregularities.

All Latin masculines ending in **or** became feminines in
French : **dolórem,** *douleur ;* **errórem,** *erreur ;* **calórem,**
chaleur ; **amórem,** *amour.* This feminine vexed the Latinists of the sixteenth century ; and as they preferred Latin to
French, they tried to turn all these words into masculines,
le douleur, le chaleur, &c. This attempt failed, as it de-
served, except in the cases of *honneur* and *labeur,* which are
masculine, and of *amour,* which has both genders[2].

---

[1] P. Meyer, *Étude sur l'histoire de la langue française,* pp. 31,
32 ; Littré, p. 106.   [2] Littré, p. 106.

. *Hymne* was originally masculine, and the feminine use of it (in speaking of church hymnology) has nothing to justify it either in etymology or in the history of the word.

Gens is properly feminine, and the idea it expresses (of men or individuals) is properly masculine; consequently this word has both genders. But it may be said generally that these distinctions of words, sometimes masculine and sometimes feminine (as *automne, gens, &c.*), and of words masculine in the singular, feminine in the plural (as *amour, orgue, délices, &c.*) are mere barbarisms and idle subtleties invented by grammarians, not arising from the historical growth of the language.

SECTION III.

NUMBERS.

French, like Latin and Aeolian Greek[1], has two numbers, singular and plural. Of these, the latter is distinguished from the former by the addition of the letter *s*. And how is this? If we consider Modern French by itself, without referring back to its 'origines,' we find it impossible to understand why it has chosen this letter to indicate the plural of nouns. It certainly looks as if it were an arbitrary choice, and as if any other letter might have done as well; and one might be tempted to see in this choice nothing but an agreement among grammarians to establish the distinction between singular and plural in this particular way; by making, in fact, a distinction which appeals to a Frenchman's eyes and not to his ears, as in most cases the *s* is mute. But in reality there is good reason for this *s*; and if we pass from Modern to Old French, we shall see what

---

[1] The Aeolian, unlike the other Greek dialects, had no dual.

it is[1]. We shall there find, it will be remembered, a declension with two cases:

SINGULAR.		PLURAL.	
murs	murus	*mur*	muri
mur	murum	*murs*	muros.

We know that in the fourteenth century the subjective case was suppressed, in both numbers, and the objective retained (*mur*, murum; *murs*, muros). Whence it, came that (taking *mur* as the type of the singular, and *murs* of the plural) the letter *s* became the characteristic of the plural. Had the language followed the contrary course, and retained the subjective case, we should have had *s* as the characteristic of the singular.

Certain substantives, like vitrum, glacies, &c., which had no plural in Latin, have one in French; as *verres*, *glaces*, &c. Others which had no singular in Latin, also have both numbers in French: as *menace*, minaciae; *noce*, nuptiae; *relique*, reliquiae; *gésier*, gigeria; *arme*, arma; *geste*, gesta, &c.

Others, again, which had both numbers in Latin, have only the plural in French: *mœurs*, mores; *ancêtres*, antecessor; *gens*, gens. As late as the seventeenth century *gens* and *ancêtres* had a singular, as we see from a couplet of Malherbe:

　　'Oh! combien lors aura de veuves
　　' *La gent* qui porte le turban';

and La Fontaine has '*la gent* trotte-menue.' *Ancêtre* was employed as a singular throughout the middle ages, and even by Voltaire, Montesquieu, and Chateaubriand. The same is true of the word *pleurs*. Bossuet followed the seventeenth century when he wrote '*le pleur* éternel.'

---

[1] Littré, ii. 357.

CHAPTER II.

THE ARTICLE.

There is no article in Latin; and, though Quinctilian pretended that the language lost nothing thereby[1], it is certain that this was a real deficiency, and that, in order to supply it, the Romans often used the demonstrative pronoun **ille**, for the sake of distinctness, where the French now has *le, la, les*. There are plenty of examples: Cicero says, 'Annus **ille** quo;' 'Ille alter;' '**Illa** rerum domina fortuna.' Apuleius has 'Quorsum ducis asinum **illum**?' Jerome writes, 'Vae autem homini **illi** per quem,' &c.

Though not rare in classical Latin, this usage is infinitely more common in the popular Latin, especially after the reduction of the six cases to two[2]; a change which made the use of an article necessary. Popular Latin appropriated to this use the pronoun **ille**: 'Dicebant ut **ille** teloneus de **illo** mercado ad **illos** necuciantes[3].' This pronoun thus transformed, and also reduced to two cases, became in Old French as follows:—

	SINGULAR.			
	MASC.		FEM.	
Subject	ille	*li*	illa	*la*
Object	illum	*le*	illam	*la*

	PLURAL.			
Subject	illi	*li*	illae	*les*
Object	illos	*les*	illas	*les*

---

[1] He says, 'Noster sermo articulos non desiderat' (*De Instit. Orat.* i. 4). Of all the Indo-Germanic languages, Greek and the Teutonic languages alone have an article. Latin and Sclavonic had none; Sanskrit only a rudimentary one.

[2] About the fifth century. See above, p. 89.

[3] From a chartulary of the seventh century.

So they said, distinguishing carefully between the two cases :

    ' Ille caballus fortis '   ' Li chevals est fort '
    ' Illum vidi caballum '   ' J'ai vu le cheval.'

And consequently, when, in due time, the subjective case disappeared, the masculine article became *le*, illum, and *les* illos, and the feminine *la*, illam, and *les*, illas. Thus we get to the modern article[1].

Combined with the prepositions *de*, *à*, *en*, the masculine article in Old French gives us :—

SINGULAR.

1. *del* (*de le*), which became *deu*[2], and thence *du*, as now.
2. *al* (*à le*),   ,,   *au*, as now.
3. *enl* (*en le*), which has disappeared.

PLURAL.

1. *dels* (*de les*), which became *des*.
2. *als* (*à les*),   ,,   *aux*.
3. *es* (*en les*), which has disappeared, with the exception of a few traces, as in *maître-ès-arts, docteur-ès-sciences, ès-mains, S. Pierre-ès-liens*.

---

[1] The reader has doubtless noticed that the article is a remarkable exception to the rule of the continuance of the Latin accent in French. M. G. Paris explains this difficulty thus :— ' The Latin comic writers reckon the first syllable of ille, illa, illum, as short ; and these words may be regarded simply as enclitics, as is shewn by the compound ellum = en illum. Had the accent been marked, the first syllable would never have been shortened or suppressed in composition. Consequently it is not wonderful that, by a solitary exception, the French language has retained only the latter syllable of this word ; il-le = *le*; il-la = *la*; il-li = *lui*; il-los = *les*.'

[2] For this softening of the final *l* into *u*, see above, p. 53.

CHAPTER III.

THE ADJECTIVE.

SECTION I.

QUALIFYING ADJECTIVES.

§ 1. *Case and Number.*

Adjectives in Old French followed the same rules of declension as substantives, and had at first two distinct cases :—

	SINGULAR.	PLURAL.
Subjective	bon-us = *bons*	boni = *bon*.
Objective	bonum = *bon*	bonos = *bons*.

They also followed the same course in the fourteenth century, abandoning the subjective case. We need not therefore reproduce the rules given above (pp. 92–95), which the student may apply for himself to the adjective.

§ 2. *Genders.*

We have laid it down as a general principle, that at the outset French grammar is nothing but a continuation of Latin grammar; consequently French adjectives follow the Latin ones in every way. Those adjectives which in Latin had two different terminations for the masculine and the feminine (as **bonus, bona**) used also to have two in French; and those which had only one termination for these genders in Latin (as **grandis**) had but one in French also. Thus in the thirteenth century men said 'une *grand* femme, une âme *mortel*,' &c. The fourteenth century, not understanding the reason of this distinction, supposed it to be a mere irregularity, and accordingly, in defiance of etymology, reduced this second class of adjectives to the form of the first class, and wrote *grande, cruelle, mortelle,* &c., to correspond to *bonne,* &c.   A trace of this older form remains in the expressions *grand'mère, grand'route, grand'-faim, grand'garde, grand'hâte, grand'chère,* &c.— phrases which are relics of the older language.   Vaugelas and the seventeenth-century grammarians, ignorant of the historic ground for this usage, decreed with their usual pedantry and dullness, that this form came from the euphonious suppression of the *e,* and that the omission must be noted by an apostrophe.

§ 3. *Adjectives used as Substantives.*

Certain words, now substantives in French, but springing from Latin adjectives, *domestique,* domesticus ; *sanglier,* singularis ; *bouclier,* buccularius ; *grenade,* granatum ; *linge,* lineus ; *coursier,* course, &c., were adjectives in Old French, following their Latin origin.   In Old French the phrase ran thus :—

Un serviteur domestique, i.e. a man attached to the service of the house (domus).   In Old French (with the usual regularity of formation) it was written *domesche,* so as not to neglect the Latin accent (domésticus).

Un porc sanglier, porcus singuláris, a wild pig, which is of solitary habits.

Un écu bouclier, clypeus bucculárius, literally an arched or bowed shield (or *buckler*).

Une pomme grenade, pomum grenátum, i. e. a fruit filled with pips or seeds.

Une vêtement linge, vestimentum lineum, i. e. a linen robe[1].

---

[1] For the change from *lineus* to *linge,* i. e. of *-eus* to *-ge,* see p. 66.

Un cheval coursier, i. e. a horse kept for racing only, as opposed to carriage-horses, &c.

In these expressions the epithet has in course of time ejected the substantive, and has taken its place. Then people began to , say, 'un *domestique*,' 'un *sanglier*,' &c., just as one now speaks of 'un *mort*,' meaning 'un homme mort,' 'un *mortel*,' for 'un être mortel,' &c.

§ 4. *Degrees of Comparison.*

In this, as in all other parts of French declension, particles have taken the place of the inflections -or, -imus, which mark in the Latin the degrees of comparison. Here, as elsewhere, we may note the analytic tendencies of the Romance tongues.

I. The COMPARATIVE is formed by the addition of the adverbs *plus, moins, aussi*, to the positive, in both Old and Modern French.

There is one peculiarity of the Old French which must be noted : beside the form *plus . . . que*, it possessed, like the Italian, the form *plus . . . de* — 'il est plus grand *de* moi.' It would do equally well to say, 'il est plus grand *de* moi,' or 'il est plus grand *que* moi;' just as, in Italian, we have 'più grande *del* mio libro.'

Some French adjectives have kept the Latin synthetic form; as *meilleur*, meliórem. As the accent is displaced in the objective case (mélior, meliórem), there has arisen (as we have seen) a declension with two cases, which are resolved either into a single case, or into the retention of the two cases with different significations. The five adjectives *bon, mal, grand, petit, moult*, have retained the old comparatives.

1. *Bon :* O. Fr. *mieldre*, mélior; *meilleur*, meliórem,
2. *Mal :* *pire*, péjor; O. Fr. *pejeur*, pejórem.
3. *Grand :* *maire*, májor; *majeur*, majórem.
4. *Petit :* *moindre*, mínor; *mineur*, minórem.

5. *Moult*, multus; *plusieurs*, pluri**ó**res.

The forms derived from the neuter are *moins*, minus; *pis*, pejus; *plus*, plus; *mieux*, melius (O. Fr. *miels*).

.We may add s**é**nior to this list; s**é**nior has given us the O. Fr. *sinre*[1], and seni**ó**rem gives us *seigneur*.

II. The SUPERLATIVE is formed by adding *le plus*, or *très*, to the positive. But in Old French '*moult* (multum) *beau*' was as correct as *très-beau*.

Some Latin superlatives lingered on into Old French. In the twelfth century men said, *saint-isme*, sanctissimus; *alt-isme*, altissimus. These vanished in the fourteenth century. The words ending in *issime*[2], &c., which are still found in French, are technical terms, not older than the sixteenth century: like all words which do not come from the popular and spontaneous period of the language, they are very ill-formed, and break the law of accent: *generalissime, reverendissime, illustrissime*, &c.

SECTION II

NOUNS OF NUMBER.

§ 1. *Cardinals.*

Unus and **duo**, which are declined in Latin, passed through the same changes in Old French as did substantives

---

[1] This word *sinre* has passed into *sire*, just as *prins* (Lat. prehensus) has become *pris*.

[2] Six centuries before the birth of the French language, the superlative had already been contracted, in common Latin, to ismus from issimus, showing the growing energy and influence of the Latin accent. The 'Graffiti' of Pompeii and the inscriptions of the earlier Empire give us **carismo, dulcisma, felicismus, splendidismus, pientismus, vicesma,** &c., for **carissimo, dulcissima, felicissima, splendidissimus, pientissimus, vicesima,** &c.

and adjectives of quality. They had two cases down to the end of the thirteenth century.

| Subject | *uns* | unus | *dui* | duo |
| Object | *un* | unum | *deux* | duos. |

The phrase then ran thus:—'*Uns* chevals et *dui* bœufs moururent' (unus caballus et duo boves): and again, 'il tua *un* cheval *et deux* bœufs' (unum caballum et duos boves).

In the fourteenth century the subjective case was lost, and here, as elsewhere, the objective remained in force.

There is nothing in particular to be said about the numbers *trois*, tres; *quatre*, quatuor; *cinq*, quinque; *six*, sex; *sept*, septem; *huit*, octo (O. Fr. *oit*[1]); *neuf*, novem; *dix*, decem.

In the words *onze*, úndecim; *douze*, duódecim; *treize*, trédecim; *quatorze* quatuórdecim; *quinze*, quíndecim; *seize*, sédecim, the position of the tonic accent has brought about the disappearance of the word decem, which gave their real force to the words úndecim, duódecim, &c.[2]

The words which serve to mark the decades,—*vingt*, vigínti; *trente*, trigínti; *quarante*, quadragínta; *cinquante*, quinquagínta; *soixante*, sexagínta; *septante*, septuagínta; *octante*, octogínta; *nonante*, nonagínta,—in which the Latin g has disappeared, were originally *véint*, *tréante*, *quaréante*, &c., whence came the modern contracted form *vingt*, *trente*, *quarante*, &c.

Above one hundred, to express the *even* decades (120, 140, 160, &c.), Old French used multiples of twenty, and wrote *six-vingt* (120), *sept-vingt* (140), &c. - meaning six times, seven times, &c. twenty; just as to this day 'eighty' is expressed by *quatre-vingt*, (4 × 20). Traces of this ancient

---

[1] Octo = *huit*; for the change of ct into it see above, p. 50.
[2] See G. Paris, *Accent latin*, p. 61.

usage remain even in our day, as in the hospital ' des *Quinze-Vingts*' (15 × 20 = 300), which was founded to support 300 blind persons; so also Bossuet and Voltaire wrote, 'il y a *six-vingts* ans.'

The Latin **ambo** (= two together) produced in Old French the adjective *ambe ;* and the phrases ran, '*ambes* mains,' '*ambes* parts,' instead of 'les deux mains,' 'les deux parts:' and the word still survives at the gaming-table, 'j'ai gagné un *ambe* à la loterie;' that is to say, 'I have won a pair,' i. e. on two figures.

§ 2. *Ordinals.*

With the exception of *premier*, **primarius**; *second*, **secundus**, which come straight from the Latin, all the French ordinals are formed by the addition of the suffix *-ième*, -**ésimus**, to the corresponding cardinals : deux-*ième*, trois-*ième*, &c.

But the system adopted in Old French for the first ten ordinals differed from that now in use. They were drawn straight from the Latin, instead of being formed from the French cardinals : thus it had *tiers*, **tértius**, instead of *trois-ième ;* *quint*, **quintus**, instead of *cinquième*. These ten ordinals, *prime*, **primus**; *second*, **secundus**; *tiers*, **tertius**; *quart*, **quartus**; *quint*, **quintus**; *sixte*, **sextus**; *setme*, **séptimus**; *oitave*, **octavus**; *none*, **nonus**; *disme* or *dîme*, **décimus**, have had interesting fortunes of their own in the history of the French tongue :—

Prime, **prímus**. This word, which has been supplanted by its diminutive *premier*, **primárius**, survives still in the phrases '*prime*-abord,' '*prime*-saut,' 'parer en *prime*,' &c.

Second, **secundus**, has not been suppressed by *deuxième*, but has a concurrent existence.

Tiers, **tértius**, remains in '*tiers*-état,' '*tiers*-parti,' and (in the feminine) in '*tierce*-personne,' 'parer en *tierce*.'

Quart, quártus, remains in ' fièvre-*quarte.*' So late as the seventeenth century, La Fontaine wrote

'Un *quart* voleur survint,'

where *quart* represents the modern *quatrième.*

Quint, quíntus. 'Charles-*Quint,*' for 'Charles *le cinquième ;*' ' la *quinte* musicale ;' and the word *quintessence* (quinta essentia) formerly written '*quinte*-essence,' is a term of alchemy, signifying the highest degree of essence, or of distillation.

Sixt, sextus. ' La *sixte* musicale,' &c.

Setme, séptimus, has disappeared altogether, giving place to *septième.* So too *oitave,* octávus, is lost, and *huitième* fills its place. The word *octave* is modern and Italian.

None, nonus. In the middle ages the ordinals marked the hours : 'il est *prime,*' 'il est *tierce,*' 'il est *dîme,*' for one, three, ten, o'clock Traces of this way of reckoning survive in the Breviary, in which there are different prayers marked off to be recited at *prime* or at *none,* i. e. at the first or ninth hour of the day.

Dîme, décimus. 'Le *dîme* jour,' 'la *dîme* heure,' were phrases used in the twelfth century for 'le *dixième* jour,' &c. So also 'la *dîme* des récoltes,' for 'la *dixième* (partie) des recoltes.'

CHAPTER IV.

PRONOUNS.

Before beginning a detailed examination of the six classes of pronouns (i. e. the Personal, Possessive, Demonstrative, Relative, Interrogative, and Indefinite), it should be noticed that here also, as before, the Old French had a declension in two cases, distinguishing subject from object, down to the close of the thirteenth century, and also that, here as elsewhere, the objective case has alone survived.

SECTION I.

PERSONAL PRONOUNS.

The Latin personal pronouns gave to Old French the following forms :—

CASE.	1st Pers.		2nd Pers.		3rd Pers.			
Sing.								
Subjective .	**Ego**	*je*	**tu**	*tu*	**ille**	*il*	**illa**	*elle.*
Obj. direct .	**Me**	*me*	**te**	*te*	**illum**	*le*	**illam**	*la.*
Obj. indirect	**Mî**	*moi*[1]	**tibi**	*toi*	**illi**	*lui.*		
Plur.								
Subjective .	**Nos**	*nous*	**vos**	*vous*	**illi**	*ils.*		
Obj. direct .	**Nos**	*nous*	**vos**	*vous*	**illos**	*ils*[2]	**illas**	*elles.*

[1] *Moi*, mî; *toi*, tibi; *soi*, sibi, were *mi, ti, si* in the eleventh century. To this form the suffix *en* was attached, and the possessives *mi-en, ti-en, si-en* formed. Unlike Modern French, the possessive pronouns in Old French were followed by the object possessed: thus they said 'le *mien* frère,' 'la *mienne* terre,' 'un *tien* vassal,' &c. This rule died out in the fourteenth century; but some relics of it remain in the following expressions: 'un *mien* cousin,' 'le *tien* propre,' 'une *sienne* tante,' &c.

[2] *Illos* is also the parent of *eux*, which was *els* in the thirteenth century, and earlier still was *ils*.

Down to the end of the thirteenth century the declension in two cases was carefully followed: *je*, ego, *tu*, tu; *il*, ille, expressed the subject only; *me*, me; *te*, te; *le*, illum, the direct object, *moi*, mihi, mi; *toi*, tibi; *lui*, illi, the indirect object. Modern French, by a strange mistake, says '*moi* qui lis,' '*toi* qui chantes,' '*lui* qui vient,' using the object for the subject; but Old French said, correctly, '*je* qui lis,' ego qui lego; '*tu* qui chantes,' tu qui cantas; '*il* qui vient,' ille qui venit, &c. It was not till the beginning of the fourteenth century that the distinction between sub-ject and object began to grow dim, and confusion arose: now we have no longer any forms peculiar to the subject, since in certain cases we express it by *je, tu, il*, in others, by *moi, toi, lui*. There is a fragment of the ancient use in the commercial phrase '*Je*, soussigné, déclare,' &c.

Though the formation of the personal pronouns offers no peculiar difficulties, we will say a few words about their origin and development.

1. *Je* and ego, which seem so far apart, are really one and the same word. *Je* is *jo* in MSS. of the thirteenth cen-tury[1]. In the tenth century it is *io*, and in the famous oaths of A. D. 842, we find the form *eo*; as '*eo* salvarai cest meon fradre Karlo,' ego salvabo eccistum meum fratrem Karolum. Here ego has lost its g and become *eo* (just as ligo becomes *lie*; nego, *nie*; nigella, *nielle*; gigantem, *géant*, &c.). There are numerous examples of the change of *eo* into *io*[2]: *io* be-comes *jo*, as Divionem becomes *Dijon*, gobionem, *goujon*[3].

2. *En*. The Latin inde obtained, in common Latin, the sense of ex illo, ab illo; as in Plautus, Amphytr. 1. 1, we have

'Cadus erat vini; *inde* implevi Cirneam.'

In Low Latin this use of inde became very common, and

---

[1] In Villehardouin, for example.   [2] See above, p. 66.
[3] See above, p. 65.

examples are plentiful in MSS. of the Merovingian period:
' Si potis **inde** manducare,' = ' si tu peux *en* manger,' occurs
in a formula of the seventh century: ' Ut mater nostra
ecclesia Viennensis in**de** nostra haeres fiat' (in a diploma
of the year 543 A.D.), &c. **Inde** then became *int* in very
early French (as is found in the oath of A.D. 842): in the
tenth century it is *ent*[1] in the twelfth *en*.

3. *Y* was in Old French *i*, originally *iv*[2], which is simply
the Latin **ibi**, a word often used in common Latin for **illi**,
illis: ' Dono **ibi** terram ;' ' tradimus **ibi** terram' (in a
chartulary of A.D. 883). The change of *b* into *v* (*iv* from
ibi) is no difficulty; it occurs in *couver* from **cubare**, *livre*
from **libra** or **liber**, *fève* from **faba**, &c.

SECTION II.

POSSESSIVE PRONOUNS.

In the Old French declension these were as follows :—

SINGULAR.

Subjective meus, *mis;* mea, *ma.*
Objective   meum, *mon;* meam, *ma.*

PLURAL.

Subjective mei, *mi';* meae, *me.*
Objective meos, *mes;* meas, *mes*[3].

In the fourteenth century this declension faded out (for
reasons explained elsewhere), and the subjects *mis*, **meus**;

---

[1] This form *ent* is retained in the word *souvent*, derived from
the Latin **subinde**.

[2] In the oaths of A.D. 842, 'in nulla adjudha contra Lodhuwig
nun li *iv* er ;' that is to say in the Latin of the day, 'in nullam
adjutam contra Ludovicum non illi ibi ero.'

[3] The same formula holds good for *ton, ta, tes,* and for *son,
sa, ses. Leur*, which comes from **illorum**, was indeclinable, and
rightly so: in Old French men said ' *leur* terres,' **illorum terrae**,
in accordance with the laws of etymology. The form *leurs* is
quite modern and illogical.

mi, mei; *me*, meae, disappeared, leaving only the objectives *mon*, meum; *ma*, meam; *mes*, meos.

Alongside of this necessary and regular change a violent disturbance took place in the fourteenth century. Old French, imitating the Latin, had a distinct pronoun for each gender; *mon*, meum, was masculine only; *ma*, meam, feminine only: before such substantives as began with a vowel, *ma* became *m'*, just as *la* became *l'*; and *m'espérance* stood for *ma espérance*, like *l'espérance* for *la espérance*. *Ta* and *sa* likewise became *t'* and *s'*: *t'amie* and *t'âme*, for *ta amie* and *ta âme*. This distinction, which was clear, convenient, etymologically just, and founded on a proper acquaintance with the language, disappeared at the end of the fourteenth century. In the next century men had ceased to say *m'âme*, *t'espérance*, *t'amie*, and had begun to say, as now, *mon âme*, *ton espérance*, *ton amie*, attaching, by a disgraceful error, the masculine pronoun *mon*, meum, to a feminine noun. This solecism has survived to this day, and the construction of Old French has fallen into oblivion[1]. 'So changes come; and now our ears would be as much astonished to hear the expression *m'espérance*, as those of a man of the twelfth century would be to hear us say *mon espérance*. And we may add that he would have the logic of grammar on his side, while we have on ours nothing but the brutal sanction of custom. The more you ascend towards antiquity, the more exact and sure does the logic of grammar shew itself to be; but, in saying this, I do not mean to deny that a tongue which necessarily, as it goes, loses on the side of exactitude, can more than make up for its losses by other qualities. Nor do I mean to say

---

[1] It has however survived in the expression *m'amour*: 'Allez, *m'amour*, et dites à votre notaire qu'il expédie ce que vous savez' (Molière, *Malade Imaginaire*, iii. 2). So also the term of endearment *m'amie*.

that I protest against the actual usage of the language, or that I am an inexorable grammarian, who wants all solecisms destroyed, and the old exactitude and regularity restored in their place[1].'

SECTION III.

DEMONSTRATIVE PRONOUNS.

The French demonstrative pronouns are three in number, *cet, celui*, and *ce*, which are combined with the two adverbs *ci* and *là*.

1. *Ce.* In the thirteenth century *ço;* in the eleventh *iço;* that is to say, ecce-hoc.

2. *Cet.* In Old French *cest;* farther back *cist;* in the twelfth century *icist;* that is to say, ecciste, = ecce-iste.

3. *Celui.* In Old French *celui* is the objective case of *cel* or *cil*, which, farther back, was *icil;* that is to say, eccille, = ecce-ille. This is all that need be said as to their etymology[2].

As to their meaning, *cist* or *cest* or *cet* answered to the Latin hic, and indicated the nearer object; *cil, cel*, or *celui* answered to ille, and indicated the more distant object. Thus, in a fable of La Fontaine (iii. 8), the lines

> ' Vivaient le cygne et l'oison,
> *Celui-là* destiné pour les regards du maître,
> *Celui-ci* pour son gout,'

would have run thus in the thirteenth century:

> ' Vivaient le cygne et l'oison,
> *Icil* (or *cil*) destiné pour les regards du maître,
> *Icest* (or *cest*) pour son gout.'

Finally, we may remark that the expressions *celui-ci*,

---

[1] Littré, *Histoire de la langue française*, ii. 415.
[2] *Ceux* (O. Fr. *iceux*) represents eccillos, just as *eux* (above, p. 109) represents illos.

celui-là, which replaced *icist, icil,* cannot be traced back beyond the fifteenth century[1].

SECTION IV.

RELATIVE PRONOUNS.

The relative pronouns, under which head the interrogative pronouns are included, are five in number: *qui, que, quoi, dont, quel,* with their compounds *lequel, laquelle,* &c.

1. *Qui, que, quoi,* come respectively from the Latin **qui, quam, quid.**

2. *Dont* comes from the Latin **de-unde** : **unde** became *ont* in Old French; so ʻle chemin par *ont* (= où) l'on va.' **Unde** joined to the preposition *de* became *dont,* whose literal meaning is *d'où,* ʻwhence,' as in ʻIl me demanda *dont* je venais.' *Dont* was still used in this sense up to the end of the eighteenth century : thus—

> ʻLe mont Aventin
> *Dont* il l'aurait vu faire une horrible descente.'
> > (Córneille, *Nic.* v. 2.)
> ʻRentre dans le néant *dont* je t'ai fait sortir.'
> > (Racine, *Bajaz.* ii. 1.)
> ʻMa vie est dans les camps *dont* vous m'avez tiré.'
> > (Voltaire, *Fanat.* ii. 1.)

---

[1] *Icelle* still remains in legal documents : ʻDe ma cause et des faits renfermés en *icelle*' (Racine, *Plaideurs*).

The same is true of *cettui (ce),* which is now only used in Marotic poetry (i.e. poetry written in imitation of Marot): ʻ*Cettui* Richard était juge dans Pise' (La Fontaine) ; ʻ*Cettui* pays n'est pays de Cocagne' (Voltaire). *Cettui* is the objective case of the pronoun whose nominative is *cet (cest* or *cist),* just as *celui* is the objective case of *cil.*

SECTION V.

INDEFINITE PRONOUNS.

The following are the chief indefinite pronouns.

1. *Aucun.* This word, written *alcun* in the thirteenth century, and *algun* in the twelfth, is compounded of *alques* and *un*, just as *chacun* is from *chaque un*, and *quelqu'un* from *quelque un.* In Old French *aliquis* became *alque :* aliqui ve- nerunt, *alque vinrent.* *Alque* then answers to *quelque,* and *algun* (*alqu'un*) to *quelqu'un.* The history and etymology of *aucun* shew that the word must be essentially affirmative in sense : 'Avez-vous entendu *aucun* discours qui ∶vous fît croire ?' 'Allez au bord de la mer attendre les vaisseaux, et si vous en voyez *aucuns,* revenez me le dire ;' 'Phèdre était si succinct qu'*aucuns* l'en ont blâmé[1].' *Aucun* becomes negative when accompanied by *ne :* 'J'en attendais trois, *aucun ne* vint.' But it must not be forgotten that *aucun* is in itself and properly affirmative, and answers to *quelqu'un,* 'some one.'

2. *Autre,* in Old French *altre,* from the Latin alter. We have seen (above p. 113) that *celui* was the complement of *cil,* *cettui* of *cet :* so also *autrui* was the complement of *autre,* and meant strictly *de l'autre ;* but according to the rule of the Old French it had no article ; people said *le cheval autrui,* or rather *l'autrui cheval,* alterius equus, for 'le cheval d'un autre.'

3. *Chaque.* The successive forms of this word are, in the thirteenth century, *chasque,* and earlier *chesque,* which is in fact the Latin quisque, *quesque, chesque.* By the addition of the word *un,* we get the compound *chasqu'un,* which as

----

[1] La Fontaine, *Fables,* vi. 1.

early as the fourteenth century was written *chacun,* and represents the Latin **quisque-unus.**

4. *Maint,* which means 'numerous,' comes from the German *manch* [1], with the same sense.

5. *Même.* The history of this word is a very curious example of the contraction undergone by Latin in its passage into French. *Même* in the sixteenth century was written *mesme,* in the thirteenth *meesme* and *meïsme,* and originally *medisme.* Now *medisme* is from the common Latin **metipsimus,** which is used by Petronius, and is a contraction of the superlative **metipsissimus,** which is found in classical Latin under the form of **ipsissimusmet,** meaning 'altogether the same.' Under the head of superlatives (p. 105), we have seen how the suffix **issimus** became **ismus** in common Latin, and provided the Old French with the superlative termination *isme.*

6. *Nul,* from the Latin **nullus,** had for its accusative *nullui,* like *cel, cet, autre,* with their objectives *celui, cettui, autrui.*

7. *On,* in the twelfth century *om,* earlier, *hom,* is simply **homo,** and means properly 'a man.' ' *On* lui amène son destrier,' i. e. 'A man brings him his war-horse.'

At first the two senses (*homme* and *on*) were not distinguished, and *om* stood for both. In the sense of **homo** the phrase ran, 'li *om* que je vis hier est mort'; and in the sense of **dicitur,** 'li *om* dit que nous devons tous mourir.' In Modern French the first example would run, ' *l'homme* que je vis,' &c.; the second would be ' *l'on* dit,' &c.

Thus, as we see, *on* was originally a substantive; whence it follows that there is nothing remarkable in its taking the article, as in *l'on.*

---

[1] The old forms of this word are the Gothic *manags,* and the Old High German *manac.*

8. *Plusieurs*, side by side with which the form *plurieurs* existed, comes from the Latin **pluriores.**

9. *Quant.* The Latin **quantus, a,** gave the Old French pronoun *quant, e.* The feminine form has fallen out of Modern French, except in the phrase, 'toutes et *quantes* fois.'

10. *Quelque.* From the Latin **qualisquam.**

11. *Quiconque*, from **quicumque.**

12. *Quelconque*, from **qualiscumque.**

In the middle ages the expression *quelque ... que* was unknown, and instead of it *quel ... que* was used (with better reason): 'A *quelle* heure *que* je vienne, je ne puis vous rencontrer,' which would now be '*à quelque* heure *que* je vienne,' &c. The older phrase is logical, the modern a barbarous pleonasm.

13. *Tel* comes from the Latin **talis.**

14. *Tout*, O. Fr. *tot*, from the Latin **totus.**

15. *Un.* In classical Latin the noun of number **unus** was used pleonastically to express 'a certain'; so Plautus says, '**Una** aderit mulier lepida'; '**Unum** vidi mortuum afferri'; and, 'Forte **unam** adspicio adolescentulam.' In all these cases **unus** bears the sense of **quidam** ; and this is also the proper sense of the French *un.*

16, 17. For *personne* and *rien*, see below, p. 162.

PART II.

CONJUGATION OF VERBS.

PRELIMINARY.

'Conjugation has perhaps been handled more freely by the Romance languages than any other part of grammar; they have remodelled it most completely. Voices have been lost, moods and tenses have disappeared, and others, which the mother tongue would not have recognised, have been created in their room; the conjugations have been thrown together and classified again upon new principles; and, in fact, the old fabric has been completely decomposed and a new structure raised out of its *débris* [1].'

The changes of the Latin conjugation, as to voice, mood, tense, and person, will be studied in detail in subsequent chapters: at present we will only glance summarily at all these transformations.

I. VOICE. To say nothing of the creation of auxiliary verbs, the most serious change has been the loss of the passive voice. The Latin passive has been suppressed, and in its room we have a combination of the verb *être* with the past participle. We find that this transformation had already taken place in common Latin; MSS. of the sixth century are full of expressions like the following:—'Ut ibi luminaria debeant *esse procurata*' (for *procurari*); 'Hoc volo *esse*

---

[1] G. Paris, *Accent latin*, p. 63.

donatum' (for *donari*); 'Quod ei nostra largitate *est con-
cessum'* (for *conceditur*). These examples are taken at
random from Merovingian chartularies and diplomas.

Deponent verbs, as they passed into French, assumed an
active form; or, to speak more correctly, had already lost
the deponent form in common Latin, and indeed even in
the Latin comic writers, who, as is well known, used many
of the forms current in the common Latin. In Plautus
we find, for example, **arbitrare, moderare, munerare, partire, venerare,** &c., in place of **arbitrari, moderari, mu-
nerari, partiri, venerari,** &c. And in the Atellan fragments we have **complectite, frustrarent, irascere** (= **irasci**),
mirabis, ominas, &c.

This is the reason why we get the forms *suivent, naissent,*
&c., which come from **séquunt, náscunt,** &c., and not
suivónt, naissónt, which would have been the natural derivatives of **sequúntur, nascúntur**; cp. above, p. 33.

II. Moods. The supines and gerunds are gone, and
a new mood, the conditional, has been created.

III. Tenses. In these there have been two modifications:
(1) The past tenses cease to be expressed by terminations
(as **am-avi, am-averam**), and are made up of the auxiliary
avoir and the past participle (*j'ai aimé,* **habeo amatum**)[1].
(2) The future is also formed by the help of the auxiliary
avoir.

The French future does not come from the corresponding Latin tense (**am-abo**), but is formed by the suffixes *-ai,
-as, -a,* &c., attached to the infinitive of the verb: *aimer-ai,
aimer-as, aime-a,* &c.

The Latins often expressed the desire of doing some-
thing in the future by **habeo** joined with the infinitive of the

---

[1] Except in the cases of the imperfect and perfect indicative,
aimais, **amabam**; *aimai,* **amavi**.

verb. Even in Cicero we have 'habeo etiam dicere'; 'ad familiares habeo polliceri'; 'habeo convenire'; 'habeo ad te scribere.' St. Augustine writes, 'venire habet' (= he will come). This form of the future ran side by side with the ordinary form in the writers of the Empire, and ended by supplanting it. From the sixth century downwards the forms 'partire habeo,' 'amare habeo,' 'venire habet in silvam,' became the more common, while the regular futures, amabo, partiar, veniet, seem almost forgotten. The Romance (or neo-Latin) languages, as they detached themselves from the mother-tongue, carried with them this new future; and retaining the inverted order of the words, amare habeo became at last aimer-ai[1]. At first the two elements were separable, and in certain neo-Latin languages, as the Provençal, their combination was not necessary; and so in Provençal je vous dirai is either 'vos dir-ai,' or 'dir vos ai.' But in French the two elements were early connected together, then became inseparable, and before long could not be distinguished.

Lacurne de Sainte-Palaye, a scholar of the last century, was the first to notice and remark on this formation of the future; and his discovery was confirmed by the later labours of Raynouard and Diez.

The French conjugations are enriched by the conditional, a mood not known to the Latins. While the Latin confounds j'aimasse and j'aimerais, under the one form amarem, the French separates these two senses and gives each its proper form. But what has been the process by which this has been arrived at?' The conditional indicates the future looked at from the point of view of the past, just as the

---

[1] In Italian the Latin habeo becoming ho, the future cantare habeo became canter-ó; in Spanish habeo = hè, and the future is cantar-é; in Portuguese habeo = hey, and the future becomes canter-ey.

future tense indicates a future looked at from the present. To express this shade of meaning the French language has created the conditional, under the form of an infinitive (*aimer*), which indicates the future, and a termination which indicates the past[1]; and hence *aimer-ais, aimer-ais, aimer-ait,* &c.

In one word, the conditional has been built on the lines of the future; but the latter has the present for its material (*aimer-ai*, &c.), the former has the imperfect (*aimer-ais*, &c.).

IV. PERSONS. Both in French and in Latin the letter *s* is characteristic of the 2nd person singular, as amas, *aimes ;* amabas, *aimais,* &c. The 1st person singular never had an *s* in Latin—amo, credo, video, teneo ; consequently, it became in Old French *j'aime, je croi, je voi, je tien.* But in the fourteenth century came in the senseless habit (senseless because not based on etymology) of adding *s* to the 1st person singular, and of saying *je vien-s, je tien-s, je voi-s.* In the eighteenth century Corneille, Molière, La Fontaine, and Racine wrote the correct form *je croi, je voi, je tien ;* and Voltaire has

     'La mort a respecté ces jours que je te *doi.*'

                      (*Alzire,* ii. 2.)

But these forms, whose historical foundation was forgotten, appeared to be nothing but poetical licences.

The letter *t* is the characteristic of the 3rd person singular: ama-t, vide-t, legi-t, audi-t, and survived in Old French *il aime-t, il voi-t, il li-t, il ouï-t,* &c. This etymological *t* disappeared from the first conjugation, but was retained in the others, *il li-t, il voi-t,* &c. It is a real grammatical mistake and misfortune that the language has thus come to neglect the primordial characteristics of the

---

[1] *-ais, -ais, -ait, -ions, -iez, -aient,* represent the Latin -abam, -abas, -abat, &c.

persons,—symbols handed down to us by tradition from
the highest antiquity. How clearly does the grammar of
the old tongue shew its regularity when compared with the
irregularities which disfigure modern grammar [1] !

V. Now that we have noted the great differences which
separate French from Latin conjugation, we cannot easily
begin the study of verbal inflexions in French without saying a few words as to the part played by the Latin accent
on French conjugation.

As regards their tonic accent, all Latin verbs may be
divided into two great classes, *strong* and *weak*, according
as the accent rests on the root (créscěre) or on the termination (amáre) : thus, créscere, dícitis, ténui in Latin (*croître,
dîtes, tins,* in French) are *strong* verbs, accented on their
root; but dormíre, debétis, amávi (*dormis, devez, aimai,* in
French) are *weak,* with the accent on their termination.

This division into weak and strong verbs, or rather into
weak and strong forms, for properly speaking there are no
completely strong verbs (i. e. verbs which accentuate the
root throughout in all tenses and persons), has thrown a
strong light on the study of French conjugation, as we
shall see in the next chapter.

The true natural classification of French verbs should
consist in their being divided into strong and weak; that
is to say, according to their *form* [2]; but rather than run
any risk of confusing the student, we will adopt the grammarians' artificial classification of verbs according to their
functions, and will divide them into Auxiliary, Active, Passive,
Impersonal, &c.

---

[1] Littré, *Histoire de la langue française,* i. 17.
[2] But even this would not be a perfect division, seeing there
are no verbs which are completely strong.

CHAPTER I.

AUXILIARY VERBS.

The most important difference between the Latin and the French conjugations lies in this,—that the passive and several past tenses of the active are expressed in Latin by terminations (**am-averam, am-or**), while in French they are expressed by the participle of the verb preceded by *avoir* for the active, and by *être* for the passive (as *j'avais aimé*, *je suis aimé*).

This introduction of auxiliary verbs in conjugation, which seems at first sight foreign to the genius of the Latin language, was not an isolated fact, or an innovation without precedents; in germ it existed in the best ages of the Roman idiom: so Cicero said, 'De Caesare satis dictum habeo' (= dixi); 'habeas scriptum .. nomen' (= scripseras); 'quae habes instituta perpolies (= instituisti). And again, Caesar, 'Vectigalia parvo pretio redempta habet (= redemit); 'copias quas habebat paratas'(= paraverat). Thus in the time of Augustus there sprang up beside the synthetic forms[1] **dixi, scripseram, paravi**, &c., the analytical form, **habeo dictum, habebam scriptum, habeo paratum**: after a time this became the form of both common Latin and of the six Romance languages; for this second form spread according as the analytical tendencies of the language developed themselves, and from the sixth century downwards Latin MSS. provide plentiful examples of it. The same is the case with the inflexions of the passive voice: common Latin substitutes for them the verb **sum**

---

[1] For the difference between *synthetic* and *analytic* forms, see Egger, *Grammaire comparée*, p. 91.

joined with the participle of the verb (sum amatus instead
of amor). In the collections of Merovingian diplomas we
meet in every page with these new forms : ' Omnia quae ibi
sunt aspecta' (= aspectantur); 'Sicut a nobis praesente
tempore est possessum' (= possidetur); 'Hoc volo esse
donatum' (= donari) ; 'Quod ei nostra largitate est con-
cessum' (= conceditur), &c.

Just as in the declensions the new languages had abandoned the terminations of the cases, and had substituted
prepositions in their room (caball-i = *du cheval*), so in the
conjugations they abandoned the synthetic forms of the
compound tenses, and replaced them by auxiliary verbs—a
natural result of that necessity which drove the Latin language from the synthetic to the analytic state.

SECTION I.

Être.

The Latin verb esse was defective, and borrowed six
tenses (fui, fueram, fuero, fuerim, fuissem, forem) from
fore and the unused fuere. In French the verb *être* is
composed of three different verbs : (1) Fuo, whence the
preterite *fus* (fui), and the subjunctive *fusse* (fuissem);
(2) Stare, which gives the past participle *été* (O. Fr. *esté*)
from status; (3) Esse, which gives all the rest of the tenses.

I. Present Infinitive: *être* (O. Fr. *estre*).

To such defective verbs as velle, posse, offerre, inferre,
esse, which were too short to carry the usual Roman infinitive, common Latin subjoined the termination -re, and so
produced a false resemblance to verbs of the second conjugation. Thus, from the sixth century downwards, Merovingian MSS. give us volere (for velle), potere (for
posse), offerrere (for offerre), inferrere (for inferre), essere
(for esse).

Essere having its accent on the first syllable (éssere) became *ess're* or *estre*, which is in fact the French infinitive. This etymology is otherwise confirmed by the form taken by the same verb in the other Romance languages; in Italian *essere*, in Spanish and Portuguese *ser*, and in Provençal *esser*. And if any one doubts whether the form essere ever did exist, we may easily reply by quoting actual cases.

Thus, in Gruter's collection of Roman inscriptions (No. 1062, 1) may be read this epitaph found in Rome in a church of the seventh century: 'Cod estis fui et cod sum essere abetis,' i. e. 'quod estis, fui, et quod sum esse habetis (= eritis). In a series of Carolingian diplomas[1], of the date A.D. 820, are these words: 'quod essere debuissent'; in the year 821, 'essere de beneficio'; in A.D. 836, 'quod de ista ecclesia Vulfaldo episcopus essere debuisset.' And the same elongation by addition of -re applied to the compounds of esse (as adesse, &c.) is also to be found; as in the Chartulary of A.D. 818, 'quam ingenuus adessere[2].'

II. PRESENT PARTICIPLE: *étant*. This is formed from *être* regularly, as *mettant* from *mettre*.

III. PAST PARTICIPLE: *été* (O. Fr. *esté*), from the Latin status.

---

[1] Pérard, *Recueil de pièces relatives à l'histoire de Bourgogne* (Paris, 1664), pp. 34–36.

[2] Perhaps it may be thought that I have insisted too much, and with two many illustrations, on the proof that *être* and *essere* are the same word. I have done so because I wished definitely to refute a widespread and often-repeated error, namely, that *être* comes from the Latin stare. How could stáre, whose accent is on the first syllable, have produced *être?* And again, how would stare go with the Provençal *esser*, the Italian *essere*, the Spanish and Portuguese *ser?* And lastly, we know with certainty that stare has become the French *ester*, and could not have produced anything else. So we have the phrase 'ester en justice,' = stare in justitia. *Ester* has also survived in a few compounds, like *rester*, re-stare; *arrêter* (O. Fr. *arrester*), ad-re-stare.

IV. Present Indicative. Comes from the corresponding Latin tense.

Suis, sum (in Old French the form was *sui,* the more correct, as there is no final *s* in the Latin); *es,* es; *est,* est; *sommes,* sumus; *êtes* (O. Fr. *estes*), estis; *sont,* sunt.

V. Imperfect. *Étais* does not come from the Latin, but has been formed straight from *être,* as *mettais* from *mettre*[1] Side by side with this imperfect of French origin, Old French had another drawn straight from the Latin : *j'ère,* eram; *tu ères,* eras; *il ert,* erat, &c. This form perished in the fourteenth century.

VI. Perfect (or definite past). From the corresponding Latin tense.

Fus (O. Fr. *fui*), fui; *fus* (O. Fr. *fuis*), fuisti; *fût,* fuit *fûmes,* fuimus (the circumflex on this word is an error of the sixteenth century, and offends against etymological propriety); *fûtes* (O. Fr. *fustes*), fuistes; *furent,* fuerunt.

VII. Future and Conditional. *Serai* (O. Fr. *esserai*) The French future is, as has been said, a compound of the infinitive of the verb and the auxiliary *avoir* (*aimerai* = amare habeo); and thus *esserai* represents essere-habeo. The same is true of the conditional *serais* (O. Fr. twelfth century, *esserais*) For the formation of the conditional, see above, p. 120.

VIII. Present Subjunctive. From the corresponding Latin tense.

Sois (O. Fr. *soi*), sim; *sois,* sis; *soit,* sit; *soient,* sint. The forms *soyons, soyez,* come from siámus, siátis, not from simus, sitis (whose resultants ought to have been *soins, soiz*)[2]

---

[1] M. Littré (*Histoire de la langue française,* ii. 201), and after him G. Paris (*Accent latin,* pp. 79, 132), have shewn that *étais* or *estois* could not possibly come from stabam. It is surely a typographical error when M. Littré, in his *Dictionnaire historique de la langue française* (s. v. *Être*), says, '*étais* vient de stabam.'

[2] See the rule for the continuance of the Latin accent, above p. 34.

IX. IMPERFECT SUBJUNCTIVE. From the Latin pluperfect. *Fusse*, fuissem; *fusses*, fuisses; *fût* (O. Fr. *fuist*), fuisset; *fussions*, fuissemus; *fussiez*, fuissetis; *fussent*, fuissent.

X. IMPERATIVE. This tense is composed entirely of forms borrowed from the subjunctive (*sois, qu'il soit, soyons, soyez, qu'ils soient*). These have been already discussed above, VIII.

SECTION II.

Avoir.

GENERAL REMARKS. The initial h of the Latin habere, *avoir*, has vanished from the French conjugation, like the h of hordeum, *orge ;* homo, *on*[1] *;* hora, *or*, &c.

The Latin b has become *v*: habere = *avoir*, habebam = *avais*, as in *prouver*, probare; *couver*, cubare; *fève*, faba; *cheval*, caballus, &c.[2]

I. PRESENT INFINITIVE. *Avoir* (O. Fr. *aver*), habére.

II. PRESENT PARTICIPLE. *Ayant*, for the Latin habéntem (or habendo). The b has disappeared in French, as *viorne*, viburnum; *taon*, tabanus, &c.

III. PAST PARTICIPLE. *Eu* (O. Fr. *eü, aü* or *aüt*); in the eleventh century *avut*, from the Latin habitum. The old form *avut* shews that, at the beginning, the French language retained the Latin b.

IV. PRESENT INDICATIVE. From the corresponding Latin tense.

Ai, hábeo; *as*, hábes; *a* (O. Fr. *at*), hábet—the *t* of the Old French being etymological; *avons* (O. Fr. *avomes*), habémus; *avez*, habétis; *ont*, hábent.

V. IMPERFECT. From the corresponding Latin tense.

Avais (O. Fr. *avoi* or *avei*), habébam (the Old French, always more correct, and true to etymology, had no *s* in the 1st person sing.); *avais*, habébas; *avait*, habébat; *avions*

(O. Fr. *aviomes*), habebámus; *aviez*, habebátis; *avaient*, habébant.

VI. PERFECT (or Preterite). From the corresponding Latin tense.

Eus (O. Fr. *eu*), hábui; *eus*, habuisti; *eut*, habuit; *eûmes* habuimus; *eûtes* (O. Fr. *eüstes*), habuistis; *eurent*, habuerunt.

VII. FUTURE AND CONDITIONAL.

Aurai, O. Fr. *avrai*, twelfth century *averai;* which is composed of the infinitive *aver* (see above, p. 119) and the auxiliary *ai*, reproducing habere-habeo; and is another instance confirming the theory of Raynouard on the formation of the future tense[1]. How useful it is to cite the Old French forms, which lie between Latin and Modern French! They illustrate the transition and shew how the passage from the one language to the other has been effected.

The conditional *aurais* (O. Fr. *avrais*), is found in the oldest texts as *averais*. For the formation of the conditional *aver-ais*, see pp. 120, 121.

VIII. PRESENT SUBJUNCTIVE. From the corresponding Latin tense.

Aie, habeam; *aies*, habeas; *ait*, habeat; *ayons* (O. Fr. *aiomes*), habeamus; *ayez*, habeatis; *aient*, habeant.

IX. IMPERFECT. From the Latin pluperfect.

Eusse, habuissem; *eusses*, habuisses; *eût* (O. Fr. *eust*, *eüst*), habuisset; *eussions*, habuissemus; *eussiez*, habuissetis; *eussent*, habuissent.

Remark.—We have seen (under III) that the past participle *eu* was originally dissyllabic *eü*, answering to its etymology. The same is true of the French imperfect. The medial *b* having disappeared, habuissem became *aüsse*, which came in the twelfth century to *eüsse*. And the *eü* of

---

[1] See above, pp. 119, 120.

eüssions, eüssiez, eüssent, &c., was both pronounced and counted in versification as two syllables.

X. IMPERATIVE. The imperative (*aïe, ayons, ayez*) is composed of forms belonging to the subjunctive. (See above, VIII.)

CHAPTER II.

CLASSIFICATION OF VERBS. CONJUGATIONS.

The French verbs, which are 4060 in number[1], are arranged under four conjugations, according to the termination of the infinitive. The first, ending in *-er,* is the largest, embracing 3620 verbs. The second, ending in *-ir,* has 350 verbs. The third, which ends in *-oir,* counts only 30, and the fourth, in *-re,* has 60. Thus the first conjugation by itself embraces nine tenths of the French verbs.

I. First Conjugation (*-er*).

The conjugation ending in *-er* answers to the Latin first conjugation in -are. As we have seen elsewhere[2], à becomes *e* in French, as nasus, *nez;* mortális, *mortel;* whence -áre = *-er,* portáre. *porter.*

At first this conjugation embraced only the Latin verbs ending in -are, and consequently has the weak infinitive, amáre, *aimer.* As time went on, learned writers introduced into this conjugation verbs derived from Latin verbs in -ere, which have no true connection with the French conjugation in *-er.*

These verbs, introduced into the French language in the fourteenth century and onwards, are of two kinds :—

1. Those from Latin verbs which have the *weak* in-

---

[1] I have based this calculation on the *Dictionnaire de l'Académie,* ed. 1835.

[2] See above, p. 67.

finitive -ēre, as persuadére, exercére, absorbére, reverére ;
these ought to have found their place in the French third
conjugation, under the forms *persuadoir, exerçoir, absorboir,
révéroir,* &c., just as habére, debére, make *avoir, devoir.*

Instead of this, which would have been the regular formation, we have the mongrel verbs *persuader; exercer, absorber,
révérer,* &c.

2. Those with the *strong* infinitive -ĕre, as afflígere, imprímere, téxere. These words answer properly to the
French fourth conjugation in -*re* (véndere, *vendre*), and
ought in French to be *afflire, empreindre, tistre*[1], not *affliger,
imprimer, tisser,* just as péndere, véndere, téndere, have
produced *pendre, vendre, tendre,* not *pender, vender, tender.*

As to verbs in -ire, there is only one such introduced into
this conjugation, namely *tousser,* tussire ; and even this one
is of modern use, for the Old French form was the correct
one, *tussir. Mouiller* and *chatouiller,* which one might be
tempted to put under this head, are not cases in point, as
they come from the common Latin forms molliare, catul-
liare, not from mollire, catulire.

II. Second Conjugation (-*ir*).

The French conjugation in -*ir* answers to the Latin fourth
conjugation ending in -īre. It embraces words derived from
Latin verbs in -ire, as finire, *finir;* in -ēre, as florére, *fleurir;*
and in -ĕre, as collígĕre, *cueillir.*

There are 350 verbs in this conjugation, which may be
subdivided under two very distinct heads :—

1. Those which follow the Latin conjugation in all their

---

[1] These verbs are not mere inventions; they are to be found
in the twelfth-century texts, instead of *affliger, imprimer, tisser.*
In fact the Dictionary of the French Academy still retains
empreindre and *tistre.*

tenses and persons: as, for example, *venir*, **venire**; whose present is *viens*, **venio**; imperfect, *venais*, **veniebam**; and so on, each French part coming directly from the corresponding Latin inflexion.

2. Those which add *-is* to the root, instead of simply following the Latin forms: as *fleurir*, **florire**; in the present *fleur-is*, imperfect *fleur-iss-ais*, instead of *fleur*, **floreo**; *fleurais*, **florebam**; which would be formed like *viens*, *venais*, from **venio**, **veniebam**. The question arises, What is the origin of these words thus strangely formed? by what procedure has the French language produced them? The answer is this: The Latins had such verbs as **durescere**, **florescere**, **implescere**, **gemiscere**, which marked a gradual growth (or augmentation) of the action expressed by the simple verb. (So **durescere** means to grow *more and more* hard.) These Priscian calls, for this reason, 'inchoative verbs.' Their characteristic syllable is **esc**, which in French became *is*: thus **flor-esc-o** became *fleur-is*; **flor-esc-ebam**, *fleur-iss-ais*, &c. The French language seized on this syllable, and added it to those Latin verbs which, when transmuted into French, would have produced forms too short and abrupt. But while it adopted this inchoative form in *iss* for the (1) indicative present, *empl-is*, **impl-esc-o**; (2) the imperfect, *empl-iss-ais*, **impl-esc-ebam**; (3) the present participle, *empl-iss-ant*, **impl-esc-entem**; (4) the subjunctive, *empl-iss-e*, **impl-esc-am**; and (5) the imperative, *empl-is*, **impl-esc-e**, it refused it for (1) the infinitive (*emplir* comes from **implere**; for **impliscere** would have produced, not *emplir* but *emplêtre*, like *paître* from **pascere**); and consequently (2) the future and (3) conditional tenses, formed as we have seen (p. 121) from the infinitive of the verb and the auxiliary *avoir* (emplir-ai), have also rejected the inchoative form. So too have (4) the perfect indicative and (5) the perfect subjunctive, which come direct from the Latin.

Thus then, to sum it up, these second-conjugation verbs are in two classes : I. The *inchoatives*, true irregular verbs, with five inchoative and five non-inchoative tenses, as we have just seen; and II. A small class of verbs which we may call *non-inchoative* (as *partir, venir*, &c.), which follow faithfully, and reproduce exactly, the Latin verb in all their tenses. At first sight one would say that these ought to be taken as the true types of the French second conjugation, and the inchoatives classed among the irregular verbs. But grammarians have followed the opposite course : the *non-inchoative* class is banished among the irregulars, and it is decided that the *inchoatives* are to furnish the typical form of the second conjugation and of its regularity. At any rate numbers are on their side. There are but 22 *non-inchoatives*, to set against 329 *inchoatives*[1].

III. Third Conjugation (-oir).

The French conjugation ending in *-oir* corresponds to that of the Latins (second), which ended in -ēre; as habēre, *avoir ;* debēre, *devoir.* This conjugation embraces only thirty French verbs; and this number may be reduced to seventeen, as the remaining thirteen are compounds.

Beside these *weak* infinitives in -ēre, certain *strong* infinitives in -ĕre have contributed to this conjugation : as recipĕre, *recevoir*, sapĕre, *savoir*, fallĕre, *falloir*, concipĕre, *concevoir*, &c.

---

[1] The following are the non-inchoatives:—*bouillir, courir, couvrir, cueillir, dormir, faillir, fuir, mentir, mourir, offrir. ouvrir, partir, guérir, repentir, sentir, sortir, souffrir, tenir, tressaillir, venir, vêtir.* Several verbs, which are at the present day solely inchoative, had in Old French simple forms which they have since lost. Thus we find in Old French *ils emplent*, implent, instead of *ils emplissent*, implescunt; *ils gèment*, gemunt, instead of *ils gém-iss-ent*, gemescunt; *gémant*, gementem, instead of *gém-iss-ant*, gemescentem, &c.

IV. Fourth Conjugation (*-re*).

This conjugation, answering to the Latin *strong* (third) conjugation in -ĕre, includes sixty verbs. It ought properly to embrace only such as are derived from *strong* Latin verbs (as légĕre, *lire;* deféndĕre, *défendre*); but through a misplacement of the accent it has come to include a number of *weak* verbs, as ridēre, respondēre, tondēre, mordēre, placēre, tacēre, whose French resultants ought properly to have been *ridoir, répondoir, tondoir,* &c. The accent however in these words being wrongly thrown back on the root-syllable (rídere, &c.) the resultant French verb, following the error, has become *rire, répondre, tondre, mordre, plaire, taire,* &c.

Before beginning the study of these conjugations it will be well to point out that the conjugation in *-oir* differs from that in *-re* only in the form of the infinitive :—

-oir : recev-oir, recev-ant, reç-u, reç-ois, reç-us.
-re : croi-re, croy-ant, cr-u, cr-ois, cr-us.

Such differences as these two conjugations may happen to present arise from modifications of the *root*, not from changes in *inflexion*. It is, therefore, perfectly fair to form one conjugation out of these two; and to say that the French language has three conjugations (1) in *-er*, (2) in *-ir*, (3) in *-oir*, or *-re*.

We propose to study the conjugations in detail under these three heads, and in the order here given.

TABLE OF FORMATION

OF THE

THREE FRENCH CONJUGATIONS.

FIRST CONJUGATION.		SECOND CONJUGATION.				THIRD CONJUGATION.	
		1. Non-inchoative.		2. Inchoative.			
Latin.	French.	Latin.	French.	Latin.	French.	Latin.	French.
PRESENT INDICATIVE.							
-o	-e	-io	-s	-isco-o, ésco-o	-is	-eo (as im- [pleo]	-s
-as	-es	-is	-s		-is	-es	-s
-at	-et, e	-it	-t		-it	-et	-t
-ámus	-omes, ons	-imus	-ons		-issons	-émus	-ons
-átis	-ez	-itis	-ez		-issez	-étis	-ez
-ant	-ent	-iunt	-ent		-issent	-ent	-ent
IMPERFECT INDICATIVE.							
-ábam	-ève, oie, ais	-iébam	-oie, ais	-isco-ébam	-iss-ais	-ébam	-ois, ais
-ábas	-ais	-iébas	-ais		-iss-ais	-ébas	-ais
-ábat	-ait	-iébat	-ait		-iss-ait	-ébat	-ait
-abámus	-ions	-iebámus	-ions		-iss-ions	-ebámus	-ions
-abátis	-iez	-iebátis	-iez		-iss-iez	-ebátis	-iez
-ábant	-aient	-iébant	-aient		-iss-aient	-ébant	-aient

PERFECT INDICATIVE.

-avi	-ai	-ivi	-i, is	"	"	-evi	*-i, is*
-avisti	-as	-ivisti	-is	"	"	-evisti	*-is*
-avit	-at, a	-ivit	-it	"	"	-evit	*-it*
-avimus	-âmes	-ivimus	-îmes	"	"	-evimus	*-îmes*
-avistis	-astes, âtes	-ivistis	-îtes	"	"	-evistis	*-îtes*
-averunt	-erent	-iverunt	-irent	"	"	-everunt	*-irent*

PRESENT SUBJUNCTIVE.

		-isc-am					
-em	-e	-iam			-iam	-eam	*-e*
-es	-es	-ias				-eas	*-es*
-et, e	-et, e	-iat				-eat	*-et, e*
-ions	-ions	-iamus				-eamus	*-ions*
-iez	-iez	-iatis				-eatis	*-iez*
-ent	-ent	-iant				-eant	*-ent*

IMPERFECT SUBJUNCTIVE.

-avissem	-asse, asse	-ivissem	-isse	"	"	-evissem	*-isse*
-avisses	-asses	-ivisses	-isses	"	"	-evisses	*-isses*
-avisset	-aist, ât	-ivisset	-ist, ît	"	"	-evisset	*-ît*
-avissémus	-assions	-ivissémus	-issions	"	"	-evissémus	*-issions*
-avissétis	-assiez	-ivissétis	-issiez	"	"	-evissétis	*-issiez*
-avissent	-assent	-ivissent	-issent	"	"	-evissent	*-issent*

IMPERATIVE.

-a	-e	-i	-s	"	-is	-e	*-s*

INFINITIVE.

-are	-er	-ire	-ir	"	"	-ere	*-re (oir)*

PARTICIPLE.

-antem	-ant	-iéntem	-ant	-isc-entem	-iso-entem	-entem	*-ant*
-atus	-et, é	-itus	-it, i	"	"	-etus, utus	*-ui, ut, u*

CHAPTER III.

FORMATION OF TENSES.

The foregoing two pages of tables of terminations are intended to make the formation of the three conjugations in (1) *-er*, (2) *-ir*, (3) *-oir* and *-re*, clearer to the eye, and set side by side all the tenses and persons of each mood.

Opposite each Latin form is placed the corresponding French form, and (when necessary to mark the transition) the Old French form is put between the two, in common type. Thus, when we read under the 1st plural present indicative, '*-ámus, -omes, -ons,*' it means that the Latin -ámus becomes in Old French -omes, and thence *-ons* in Modern French. Such Latin terminations as are unaccented in this table become mute in French.

Remarks.

I. PRESENT INDICATIVE.

In the second and third conjugations the *s* has been wrongly added to the 1st person sing., as *par-s, rend-s.* This letter (which violates the rules of etymology) did not exist in Old French, whose forms were *je voi, je rend ;* the *s* was properly reserved to mark the 2nd person sing., *tu rend-s*, **reddis** ; *tu voi-s*, **vid-es.** For the origin of this *s,* see above, p. 121.

The *t* which marks the 3rd person sing., **ama-t, vide-t, legi-t, audi-t,** survived throughout in O. Fr. *il aime-t*[1], *il lit, il ouït.* But through one of those strange and inconsequent changes which often meet us in the growth of languages,

---

[1] The *-et* in *aimet* is mute, like the *-ent* of *aiment.*

and not uncommonly in French, this etymological *t* disappeared from the first conjugation (*il aime*), while it remained in all the others (*il lit, voit, ouït*).

The 1st person plur. (amámus) was originally *aim-omes.* As time went on all the terminations in *-omes* were softened down into *-ons*, and the only relic of the form still to be found in Modern French is the word *sommes* (sumus), which ought to have been reduced to *sons*, just as *aim-omes* has become *aim-ons.*

The third conjugation in Latin (légĕre) had the 1st and 2nd persons plur. légĭmus, légĭtis, strong; whence the resultants ought to have been *límes, lítes*, not *lisóns, liséz*, which are weak forms. The fact is that the word came to be wrongly accented, and pronounced legímus, legítis, whence the forms *lisons, lisez*, naturally followed. *Dítes* (dícĭtis) and *faites* (fácĭtis), which are regarded as exceptions by grammarians, are in reality perfectly regular. In Old French the 1st person plur. of these same verbs was also strong, *dímes* (dícĭmus), in place of *disons*, and *faimes* (fácĭmus) instead of *faisons.*

II. IMPERFECT.

-abam became in French, following the dialects from south to north, *-ève, -oie, -eie, -oue.* Thus amabam became in Burgundy *am-ève*, in the Ile de France (or in French proper), *am-oie*, in Normandy *am-oue*[1]. The dialect of the

---

[1] Notice how near the form *amève*, which retains the Latin consonant ($v = b$) is to the original am-abam. And indeed it is generally true that the Romance forms, which are as clear and sonorous in the south as the Latin itself, contract and become dull-sounded, as one goes northward. Thus cantabam became in Spain *cantaba*, in Italy and Provence *cantava*, in Burgundy *chantève*, in the Ile de France *chantois*, in Normandy *chantoue*. Latin words are like a very sensitive thermometer : as one goes northward it drops lower and lower; but these changes take place in continued and successive descents, not by sudden falls. 'Natura nil facit per saltum.'

Ile de France having gradually supplanted all the others[1], its imperfect *-oie*, *-abam*, prevailed, and became the type of the Modern French imperfect. In the fourteenth century an erroneous *s* was subjoined to the 1st person sing., and hence we get the form *-ois* (*am-ois*), which prevailed up to the end of the eighteenth century, when Voltaire substituted for it the now established termination in *-ais* (*aim-ais*). A century before Voltaire, in the year 1675, an obscure lawyer, Nicolas Bérain, had already suggested this reform.

It may be further noticed that the 1st and 2nd persons plur. *chantions*, *chantiez*, now dissyllabic, were trisyllabic in Old French—*chant-i-óns*, canta[b]-ámus ; *chant-i-éz*, canta-[b]átis. The older form marks the force of the Latin accent.

III. PERFECT.

Cantávi, cantávit, cantávimus, have resulted regularly in *chantai, chanta, chantâmes. Chantas, chantâtes, chantèrent*, however, do not come from cantavisti, cantavistis, cantavérunt[2], but from the contracted forms cantasti, cantastis, cantarunt. For the same reason *dormis, dormîtes, dormirent*, come from dormisti, dormistis, dormirunt, not from dormivísti, dormivístis, dormivérunt.

It may also be remarked that the perfects of the first three conjugations are weak : *chant-ai*, cantávi ; *dormis*, dormívi ; *rendis*, réddidi[3]. The strong perfects, *vins*, véni ; *fis*, féci, belong to the irregular verbs.

IV. FUTURE AND CONDITIONAL.

These tenses do not appear in the Table of Formation of Tenses, because their proper place is not there. The table

---

[1] This fact is explained above, p. 19.

[2] These longer forms, following the law of the influence of the Latin accent, would have produced in French *chanteïs, chanteïstes, chanteirent*, not *chantas, chantastes, chantèrent*.

[3] For perfects of the third conjugation, see the chapter on Irregular Verbs, p. 142.

is intended to give a comparative view of those tenses which come direct from the Latin, or in other words, of the simple tenses: the future and conditional are compound tenses, made up of the infinitive of the verb and the auxiliary *avoir* (*aimer-ai, aimer-ais*).   On which point see above, p. 120.

V. Present Subjunctive.

The t which ended the 3rd person sing. of this tense in Latin ame-t, dormia-t, redda-t, &c., though now lost in the French *aime, donne, rende,* &c., was present in O. Fr. *aimet, dormet, rendet.* It survives still in the two words *ait,* habeat, and *soit,* sit.

It is now impossible to distinguish between the imperfect indicative *chantions, chantiez,* and the present subjunctive. But in Old French they were clearly distinguished; for the subjunctive forms were dissyllabic, while the imperfect indicative was trisyllabic, following the Latin accent:—

Imperf. indic. : *Chant-i-ons,* cant-ab-ámus ; *chant-i-ez,* cant-ab-átis.

Subjunct. pres. : *Chant-ions,* cant-émus ; *chant-iez,* cant-étis.

VI. Imperfect Subjunctive.

Here, as in the perfect indic. (III) the French form is derived from the contracted Latin form: *aim-asse* does not come from am-avissem, but from am-àssem.

VII. Imperative.

The 2nd person sing. is formed from the Latin imperative *aim-e,* ama; *fin-i,* finis, &c. The other persons are usually borrowed from the indicative.

VIII. Present Infinitive.

In addition to the details given in Section II we may here say that certain Latin infinitives in -ĕre (consequently *strong*), have produced *strong* infinitives in Old French, and weak ones in Modern French. Thus cúrrere, quaérere, frémere, gémere, imprímere, have resulted in O. Fr. *courre*[1], *querre*, *freindre*, *geindre*, *empreindre*, but in Modern French these have become *courir*, *quérir*, *frémir*, *gémir*, *imprimer ;* these forms arising from a misplacement of the Latin accent.

IX. Present Participle.

The French language has adopted the form of the objective case, am-ántem, *aimant*[2]*;* not of the subjective, amans.

X. Past Participle.

All the past participles of what are called regular verbs are weak: *aim-é,* amátus; *fin-i,* fin-ítus, &c. There are a few strong forms among past participles; but these belong exclusively to irregular verbs.

Originally, all past participles which were strong in Latin kept the strong form in French: thus *vendre,* vend-ere, had *veni,* not *vendu,* as its past participle. At a later period these forms were made weak by the addition of the final *u* (mark of the weak participle of the third conjunction). Then the strong forms disappeared from the ranks of participles, though a considerable number of them are still in existence as substantives.

Before leaving the past participle we may observe that the Romance languages, and especially French, possess the faculty of being able to form substantives out of past participles: we can say *un reçu, un fait, un dû*—words which are really the past participles of *reçevoir, faire, devoir.* But this is more especially the case with feminine participles as *issue, vue, étouffée, venue, avenue,* &c. The number of substantives thus added to the language is considerable; for they are formed from both classes of participles, strong and weak :—

---

[1] Still used in the phrase '*courre* le cerf.' It was in use in the eighteenth century. 'Aller *courre* fortune' is a phrase employed by Mme. de Sévigné, Bossuet, Voltaire, &c.

[2] [Or from amando, 'une femme *aimant* son mari,' 'femina amando suum maritum.']

1. With weak, or regular, participles : *chevauchée, accouchée, fauchée, tranchée, avenue, battue, crue, déconvenue, entrevue, étendue, issue, revue, tenue,* &c.

2. With strong, or irregular, participles : *un dit, un joint, un reduit, un trait,* &c.   As we have said, these forms disappeared as participles, but survive as substantives; as *vente,* vén̄dita, which is the old form of the participle, now *vendue.*

Subjoined is a list of these substantives[1]—' a list whose special interest lies in the illustration it affords of the history of the Latin accent, and of its influence at the time of the formation of the French language.'

By the side of the old strong participle, now a substantive, and the Latin word it comes from, we will place the modern weak participle in parentheses.

1. First Conjugation : *emplette,* implícita (*employée*); *exploit,* explícitum (*éploye*).

2. Third Conjugation: *meute,* móta (*mue*), and its compound *émeute,* emóta (*émue*); *pointe,* puncta (*poindre*), meaning to prick, púngere (this word has remained as a participle in the expression *courte-pointe,* O. Fr. *coulte-pointe,* Lat. cúlcita puncta); *course,* cursa (*courue*); *entorse,* intorta (*tordue*); *trait,* tractum, and its compounds *portrait, retrait,* &c.; *source* (*surgie*), and its compound *ressource,* from the verb *sourdre* (súrgere); *route,* rupta (*rompue*), and its compounds *déroute, banqueroute* (i. e. *banque rompue*); *défense,* defensa (*défendue*), and its kinsfolk *offense,* &c.; *tente,* tenta (*tendue*), and its compounds *attente, détente, entente,* &c.; *rente,* réddita (*rendue*); *pente,* péndita* (*pendue*), and its compounds, as *soupente,* suspéndita* (*suspendue*); *vente,* véndita (*vendue*); *perte,* pérdita (*perdue*); *quête,* quaésita, and its compounds *conquête, requête, enquête ; recette,* recepta (*reçue*); *dette,* débita (*díte*); *réponse,* responsa (*répondue*); *élite,* electa (*élue*).

---

[1] Or rather of such of them as offer any points of interest.

CHAPTER IV.

IRREGULAR VERBS (so called).

Grammarians have entitled the following verbs 'irregular,' and those treated of in Chapter III 'regular'; but, if proper regard be paid to the place of the Latin accent, it will be seen that we are right in calling the former verbs *strong* and the latter *weak*. The terms 'regular' and 'irregular' do but state a fact, at best; but the distinction between *strong* and *weak* penetrates deeper, and expresses a theory. Looked at from our point of view, the old conception of irregularity disappears, and the word is applied solely to anomalous and defective verbs; and the *strong* verbs (hitherto named 'irregulars') are considered simply as another method of conjugation. 'Irregularity' presupposes formations which, for whatever cause, have deviated from the typal form; but, in the case of strong verbs, no such deviation has taken place: they are as regular as any others, only they obey a different law[1].

The verbs usually styled 'regular' have a weak perfect (i.e. accented on the last syllable), as **amávi**, *aim-ái;* dormívi, *dorm-ís;* redd-ídi, *rendís*, &c., and all regular verbs of the strong type have their perfect strong (i.e. accented on the root), as ténui, *tíns;* díxi, *dís;* féci, *fís.*   -

There are only two irregular verbs under the second conjugation[2]; *tenír* from tenére, and *venir* from veníre, whose preterites are *tíns*, ténui, and *vins*, véni.

The seventeen verbs collected under the name of the third conjugation, which have vexed philosophical gram-

---

[1] Cp. Littré, *Histoire de la langue française*, i. 121.

[2] The first conjugation has no irregular verbs, properly so called; for *aller* and *envoyer* are anomalous.

marians from Vaugelas to Girault-Duvivier, are for the most part old strong verbs, like *recevoir*, recípere; *concevoir*, concípere; *decevoir*, decípere, which in Old French were *reçoivre*, *conçoivre*, *déçoivre*, following the law of their etymology. These all have the strong perfect, *reçus*, recépi; *conçus*, concépi; *déçus*, decépi.

The fourth conjugation has nine irregular verbs: *dire*, dícere; *plaire*, plácere[1]; *taire*, tácere; *faire*, fácere; *mettre*, míttere; *prendre*, préndere; *rire*, rídere; *lire*, légere; *croire*, crédere; whose perfects are the following strong forms—*dis*, díxi; *fis*, féci; *mis*, mísi; *pris*, préndi; *plus*, plácui; *tus*, tácui; *ris*, rísi; *lis*, légi, *crus*, crédidi.

CHAPTER V.

DEFECTIVE AND ANOMALOUS VERBS.

Defective verbs are those which, like *faillir*, are deficient in some tenses, moods, or persons.

Anomalous verbs are those whose irregularities forbid them to be arranged under any class. These are the true 'irregular verbs.'

SECTION I.

DEFECTIVE VERBS.

Two in the first conjugation—*ester* and *tisser;* six in the second—*faillir, férir, issir, ouïr, quérir, gésir;* thirteen in

---

[1] The accent on the verbs plácere, tácere, rídere, came at last to override the force of the long penultimate. See above, p. 133.

the third—*braire, frire, tistre, clore, soudre, sourdre, traire, paître, souloir, falloir, chaloir, choir, seoir*[1].

1. *Ester.* Used in the infinitive only in certain judicial formulæ, as '*ester* en jugement' (to bring an action, to institute a suit); 'La femme ne peut *ester* en jugement sans l'autorisation de son mari[2].' This verb, which comes from the Latin **stare** (see above, p. 125), remains still in the compounds *contraster*, contra-stare; *rester*, re-stare; *arrêter* (O. Fr. *arrester*), ad-re-stare; and in the participles *constant*, con-stare; *distant*, di-stare; *instant*, in-stare; *non-ob-stant*, ob-stare. The past participle *esté*, status, has been borrowed by the verb *être*, and contracted into *été*. See above, p. 126.

2. *Tisser* and *tistre.* These two verbs come from the Latin **téxĕre.** The strong form, *tistre*, **téxĕre**, which is the Old French one, has disappeared, leaving only its participle *tissu* (which comes from *tistre*, just as *rendu* from *rendre*). The weak *tisser* (which comes, as it were, from **texére**) violates the law of Latin accent, and is a modern word: it has prevailed over the other form, but has adopted its strong past participle.

3. *Faillir.* The three persons of the sing. *je faux, tu faux, il faut*, have almost fallen into disuse, and we may regret the fact. They remain in the phrases, 'le cœur me *faut*;' 'au bout de l'aune *faut* le drap,' i.e. 'the cloth fails at the end of the ell' = 'all things come to an end.'

The future and conditional *faudrai, faudrais*, are also being forgotten, and have been almost entirely replaced by the compounds *faillir-ai, faillir-ais*. Instead of 'je ne

---

[1] These verbs, which are now defective, had in Old French all their tenses and persons; and consequently they have no real right to form a separate class. It is in fact a *historical* accident, which may affect verbs of any conjugation.

[2] *Code Napoleon*, Art. 215.

faudrai point à mon devoir,' people now begin to say, 'je ne *faillirai* point.'

4. *Férir.* From the Latin feríre. It survives in the phrase · sans coup *férir*'—'D'Harcourt prit Turin sans coup *férir*.' In Old French this verb was conjugated throughout, and was, in the indicative present, je *fier*, fério; tu *fiers*, féris; il *fiert*, férit [1], &c.; in the imperfect *férais*, fériebam; in the participle *férant*, férientem, and *féru*, féritus, &c.

5. *Issir.* From the Latin exire (For the change of e into *i*, see p. 50; of x into *ss*, see p. 74.) In Old French this word was conjugated thus:—*is*, éxeo; *is*, éxis; *ist*, éxit; *issons*, eximus, *issez*, exitis; *issent*, exeunt. Imperfect, *issais;* future, *istrai;* participles, *issant*, *issu*, and *issi*.

6. *Ouïr.* From the Latin audíre. In Old French it was conjugated throughout, *j'ouïs*, audio; *j'oyais*, audiébam; future, *j'orrai;* participles, *oyant*, audiéntem; *ouï*, auditus.

The Old French future *orra*, now lost, was extant in the seventeenth century: Malherbe wrote—

> 'Et le peuple lassé des fureurs de la guerre
> Si ce n'est pour danser, n'*orra* plus de tambours.'

Later still, the imperfect *oyais* is playfully employed, by J. J. Rousseau in an epigram:—

> 'Par passe-temps un cardinal *oyait*
> Lire les vers de Psyché, comédie,
> Et les *oyant*, pleurait et larmoyait.'

The past participle survives in law terms [2]: '*Ouïe* la lecture de l'arrêt,' i. e. 'the reading of the judgment having been heard.'

---

[1] This word remains in a few heraldic legends. The house of Solar had as its motto, 'Tel *fiert*, qui ne tue pas.'

[2] So the Norman-French *oyez* survives in the English crier's 'O yes, O yes!' and in the law phrase '*oyer* et terminer.'

7. *Quérir.* As to this word, whose compounds are *acquérir, requérir,* and *conquérir,* see above, p. 140. The strong conjugation had *querre* as the infinitive (as may be seen as late as La Fontaine): present indic. *quiers, quérons ;* fut. *querrai ;* pret. *quis ;* p. p. *quis (requis conquis,* &c.).

8. *Gésir, gisir.* From the Latin **jacere.** The present part. of *gisir* survives, *gisant.* It has a derivative also, *gésine :* ' La laie était en *gésine* [1].'

9. *Braire.* Only used (according to the Académie Française) in the infinitive and in the 3rd persons of the present indic., *brait, braient ;* of the future, *braira, brairont ;* and of the conditional, *brairait, brairaient.* But M. Littré shews clearly that this verdict of the Academy is too severe, and he proposes to employ all the forms of this verb which existed in Old French (il *brayait,* il *a brait,* &c.). *Braire,* from the Low Latin **bragire,** a word whose derivation is obscure, bore in Old French the general sense of ' to cry out,' and was applied to man as well as to animals. It is only in later days that it has been limited to the braying of the ass [2].

10. *Frire.* From the Latin **frigere.** This verb still keeps all its tenses (*fris, frirai, frit,* &c.) except the imperfect *friais,* the particle *friant,* subjunctive *frie,* and the three persons plural of the present indicative, *frions, friez, frient* (as *rire* makes *rions, riez, rient*). All these forms are to be found in Old French.

11. *Clore.* From the Latin **claudere** : O. Fr. *clorre* shews the *d* in the first *r* (for the change from **dr** to *rr,* see above, p. 74). *Clos, clorai,* in Old French *closais, closant.* Its compounds are *éclore* (O. Fr. *esclore,* Latin **ex-claudere**), *enclore* (**in-claudere**), and the O. Fr. *fors-clore* (**foris** claudere). The form **cludere** in **ex-cludere, con-cludere, re-cludere,**

---

[1] La Fontaine, *Fables,* iii. 6.
[2] This is also true of the English verb ' to bray.'

has produced the French forms, *exclure, conclure, reclure,* whose past participle, *reclus, recluse,* still survives.

12. *Soudre* (O. Fr. *soldre,* Latin **sólvere**); like *moudre,* from **mólere.** The past participle was *sous.* The compounds *absoudre,* **absolvere**; *dissoudre,* **dissolvere**; *résoudre,* **resolvere,** also form their past participle in the same way, *absous, dissous ; résous* has given way to *résolu,* though it remains in 'brouillard *résous* en pluie,' 'fog turned into rain.'

13, *Sourdre.* From the Latin **súrgere.** The strong participle *source* (as we have seen on p. 141) has survived as a substantive, and has a compound *ressource.*

14. *Traire.* From the Latin **trahere.** In Old French this word had the same sense as the Latin verb; and it is only lately that it has been restricted to the sense of milking. Compounds—*abstraire,* **abs-trahere**; *extraire,* **ex-trahere**; *soustraire,* **sub-trahere.** In addition to these there are, in Old French, the words *portraire,* **pro-trahere**; *retraire,* **re-trahere**; *attraire,* **at-trahere,** whose participles have given us the substantives *portrait, retrait, retraite,* and the adjective *attrayant.*

15. *Paître.* O. Fr. *paistre,* Latin **páscere.** The past participle survives in the language of falconry, as *pu*—'un faucon qui a *pu,*' and in the compound *repu* from *repaître.*

16. *Souloir.* From the Latin **solére.** It had all its tenses in Old French; but is now used only in the 3rd person imperfect indicative; 'il *soulait,*' i.e. 'he was wont.' La Fontaine says in his Epitaph—

> 'Deux parts en fit, dont il *soulait* passer
> L'une à dormir, et l'autre à ne rien faire.'

17. *Falloir.* For this word, which comes from **fallere,** and only differs from *faillir* in its conjugation, see above, p. 144.

18. *Chaloir.* From the Latin **calere.** Now used only n the 3rd sing. pres. indic. : 'il ne m'en *chaut,*' = 'it does

not trouble me,' 'is no affair of mine.' Still extant in La Fontaine, Molière, Pascal : 'Soit de bond, soit de volée, *que nous en chaut-il,* pourvu que nous prenions la ville de gloire[1].' Voltaire, too, has 'Peu *m'en chaut,*' 'little care I !' In Old French this verb had all its tenses : *chalait, chalut, chaudrai, chaille, chalu*[2].

19. *Choir.* O.Fr. *chêoir,* and in very early French *chaer, caer, cader,* Lat. cádere, wrongly accented as cadére (as we have seen above, p. 133). Scarcely used except in the infinitive. But the Old French conjugated the whole verb (*chois, chéais, cherrai, chut, chéant, chu*). The future, *cherrai,* was used in the seventeenth century : 'Tirez la chevillette, et la bobinette *cherra*[3]'; also the preterite *chut:* 'Cet insolent *chut* du ciel en terre[4]'; also the participle *chu,* as in Molière, Femmes Savantes, iv. 3 :—

> 'Un monde près de nous a passé tout du long,
> Est *chu* tout au travers de notre tourbillon.'

Its compounds are *déchoir* and *échoir* (de- and ex- cadere). In Old French there was also *méchoir, mescheoir* (from minus-cadere, see below, p. 180), whose pres. part. we have still in the adjective *méchant* (O. Fr. *meschant, meschéant*).

20. *Seoir.* O. Fr. *seoir,* and in very early Fr. *sedeir,* Lat. sedere. The participles *séant,* sedentem ; *sis, sise,* situs, sita, are still in use. Compounds, *asseoir,* ad-sedere ; *rasseoir* and *surseoir,* re-, ad-, and super-sedere ; also *bien-séant, mal-séant.*

SECTION II.

ANOMALOUS VERBS.

We have already said that the anomalous are the true irregular verbs, as they cannot be brought under any common classification.

They are the following :

---

[1] *Provinciales,* Lettre ix.   [2] It survives in *non-chalant.*
[3] Perrault.   [4] Bossuet, *Démonstr.* ii. 2.

1. *Aller.* This verb has borrowed its conjugation from three different Latin verbs: (1) 1st, 2nd, and 3rd sing. pres. indic. from **vádere**—je *vais*, **vado**; tu *vas*, **vadis**; il *va* (O. Fr. *il vat*[1]), **vadit.** (2) The future and conditional (*j'irai, j'irais*) come from the Lat. **ire**, by the usual formation of the future (see pp. 119, 120). (3) All other tenses (*allais, allai, allasse, aille,* &c.) come from the same root with the infinitive *aller.* Whence then this *aller?* In Old French it was written *aler* and *aner. Aner* leads us to the Low Lat. **anare,** Lat. **adnare**[2]. (The change of **n** into *l*, **anare** to *aler*, is not uncommon, as may be seen from such forms as *orphelin* from **orphaninum,** &c., see above p. 56).

2. *Convoyer, dévoyer, envoyer, fourvoyer.* The Latin **via,** which has produced the French *voie,* formed in Low Latin a verb **viare,** whence O. Fr. *véier,* antique form of the modern *voyer,* preserved in the compounds given above. *Convoyer,* **con-viare,** to escort, travel with any one. A merchant-ship is still said to be '*convoyé* par deux vaisseaux de guerre.' *Dévoyer,* O. Fr. *desvéier,* Lat. **de-ex-viare.** It has another form in *dévier. Envoyer,* O. Fr. *entveier,* comes from **inde-viare.** *Fourvoyer,* O. Fr. *forveier,* from **foris-viare,** to go out of the way[3].

---

[1] The *t* of this form *vat* is etymologically valuable.

[2] **Adnare** and **enare,** which rightly mean 'to go by water,' soon came to express the action of coming and going in any way; whether by flying, as in Virgil (*Aen.* vi. 16), 'Daedalus . . . gelidas **enavit** ad Arctos;' or by walking, as in Silius Italicus, 'Enavimus has valles.' It is curious that this transition from sea to land has also befallen the verb *arriver.* The Low Lat. **adripare** signified originally 'to reach the shore,' of a traveller on board ship; thence it has got the wider meaning of 'attaining to any end in view,' of *arriving.* [By a reverse process the wayfaring **viaggio,** *voyage,* of Italy and France, has in the hands of the seafaring English been limited to the paths of the ocean.]

[3] It must be a typographical error that makes M. Littré derive *dévier* from **deviare,** and *envoyer* from **inviare.** He knows better than any one else the Old French forms *desvier, entvoyer,* which preclude such derivations.

3. *Bénir.* As dicere has become *dire,* benedicere became *benedir,* or *beneïr.* This, the Old French form, which shews the continuance of the tonic accent, disappears by contraction, and is replaced by the modern *bénir.*

The pretended difference set up by French grammarians between *bénite* and *bénie* is illusory, and has no foundation in the history of the language. Participles ending in *-it* (as *bénit, finit, réussit*) dropped the *t* in the fourteenth century, and *bénit* became *béni* (and *finit, réussit,* became *fini, réussi*). The form *bénit* survives in the phrases 'pain *bénit,* eau *bénite.*'

4. *Courir.* For this verb, see above, p. 140.

5. *Mourir.* From the Low Lat. morire,' which passed from the deponent to the active form, and thence into the French. See above, p. 119.

6. *Vivre.* From the Lat. **vivere.** The perf. *vécus* (O. Fr. *vescus, vesqui*), is singularly anomalous.

7. *Boire.* O. Fr. *boïvre,* Lat. **bibere.**

8. *Voir.* O. Fr. *véoir,* Lat. **vidére.** The Old French form displays the force of the Latin accent, and the loss of the medial consonant d. In eleventh-century texts the form *vedeir* is met with.

In Old French the future was *voir-ai;* and this, which is ·a better form than *verrai,* is preserved in the compounds *pour-voirai, pré-voirai,* &c. It would seem, at first sight, that *vis,* vidísti ; *vîmes,* **vidimus** ; *vîtes,* **vidistis** ; *visse,* **vidissem,** violate the law of the force of the Latin accent; but this is not so, as is shewn by the Old French forms *véis,* vidísti ; *véimes,* vídimus ; *véistes,* **vidístis** ; *véisse,* **vidíssem,** &c. The same is true of *tins,* tenuisti; *vins,* venisti; *tinnse, vinnse,* which are not exceptions to the law of accent, but contractions from Old French regular forms, *tenis,* tenuísti ; *venis,* venísti; *tenisse,* tenuíssem ; *venisse,* veníssem.

9 *Mouvoir.* The Lat. movére produced at first the form *mover* (still in use in central France), for which *mouvoir* was afterwards substituted.

10. *Savoir.* O. Fr. *saver*, Lat. sapére. This earlier form *saver* gave the future *saver-ai*, which, afterwards contracted into *savrai*, became *saurai* in the fourteenth century, just as habere produced *aver-ai*, *avrai*, *aurai*.

11. *Valoir.* From the Lat. valére. The pres. part. *vaillant* survives as an adjective.

12. *Écrire.* The O. Fr. *escrivre*, preserved the final b of the Lat. scríbere. All the anomalous forms, such as *écrivons* scribémus; *écrivais*, scribébam, are etymologically correct, and come from the corresponding Latin forms. Its compounds are *décrire*, *circonscrire*, *prescrire*, *proscrire*, *souscrire*, *transcrire*.

13. *Naître.* The common Latin converted all deponents into active verbs, as we have seen (p. 119). Thus nasci became náscere, whence *naître*, like *paître* from páscere. The barbarous perfect nascívi produced the O. Fr. *nasqui*, now *naquis.*

14. Verbs ending in *-uire*[1]. *Duire*, dúcere (in its compounds *conduire*, *déduire*, *réduire*, *induire*, *traduire*, *produire*, *introduire*), *cuire*, cóquere ; *nuire*, nócere ; *luire*, lúcere, and the compounds of *struire*, struere ; *construire*, *instruire*, *détruire*, destruere.

15. Verbs ending in *-ndre.* These verbs, whose *d* does not belong to the Latin root[2], as *ceindre*, cíngere, drop the *d* in the indic. pres. (*ceins*, *ceint*, *ceignons*, &c.), and have a strong past part. *ceint*, cínctus, which retains the Latin t. On this model are conjugated the following : *éteindre*, ex-

---

[1] All these verbs have a weak perfect, which hinders us from placing them under the irregular verbs.

[2] Thus the *d* of *rendre* (réddere) belongs to the Latin ; that of *ceindre* (cingere) does not.

stínguere ; *étreindre*, stríngere ; *contraindre*, constríngere ; *astraindre*, astríngere ; *restreindre*, restríngere ; *feindre*, fíngere ; *enfreindre*, infríngere ; *peindre*, píngere ; *plaindre*, plángere ; *teindre*, tangere ; *atteindre*, attíngere ; *joindre*, júngere, with its compound; *oindre*, úngere ; *poindre*, pungere ; *épreindre*, exprímere ; *empreindre*, imprímere ; *geindre*, gémere.

PART III.

UNDER this head we will consider the four classes of invariable words which have been handed down to us by the Latins: Adverbs, Prepositions, Conjunctions, Interjections.

Before we go through them, two remarkable facts must be noted: (1) the addition of *s* to the termination of most of the invariable words, which had no such final letter in Latin—as *tandis*, tam diu; *jadis*, jam diu; *sans*, sine, *certes*, certe, &c.; the O. Fr. *oncques*, unquam; *sempres*, semper; and (2) the suppression of the final *e* in the two substantives casa, *chez*, and hora, *or*, whose proper French forms would have been *chèse* and *ore*, just as rosa has produced *rose*. Let us add that with the exception of two adjectives, *guères* and *trop*, which come from German, all particles are of Latin origin.

CHAPTER I.

ADVERBS.

The Latin suffixes, -e, -ter, which marked the adverb (docte, prudenter, &c.), disappeared because they were not accented; and, in order to produce a class of words which should bear the grammatical mark of the adverb, the French language adopted other suffixes. It took for this purpose the substantive mens, which, under the Empire had come to mean 'manner,' 'fashion,' &c, as in Quinctilian, 'bona mente factum'; in Claudian, 'devota mente tuentur'; in Gregory of Tours, 'iniqua mente concupiscit,' &c. This ablative mente, joined with the ablative feminine of the adjective, produced the French adverbial ending *-ment :* bona-, cara-, devota-mente ; *bonne-, chère-, dévote-ment.*

But those Latin adjectives which had different terminations for masculine and feminine (as bonus, bona) had also two in French (*bon, bonne*) ; while those Latin words which had but one termination for these genders, had also only one in Old French : thus grandis, legalis, prudens, regalis, viridis, fortis, &c., became in French *grand, loyal, prudent, royal, vert, fort,* &c., which adjectives are invariable in Old French. Consequently, in the case we are studying, adverbs formed by means of the former class (such as *bon, bonne*) always retained the *e* of the feminine in their root (*bonne-ment, chèrement, dévotement*), while those formed with the latter class (*grand, royal,* &c.) never had *e* in the radical ; and accordingly, in the thirteenth century, these adverbs were *loyal-ment, grand-ment, fort-ment,* &c. But the fourteenth century, no longer understanding the origin of this distinction, and no longer seeing why, in certain adverbs, the adjective was feminine, while in others it seemed to be masculine, inserted the *e, loyal-e-ment, vil-e-ment,* &c.—barbarisms opposed both to the history of the words, and to the logical development of the language.

SECTION I.

ADVERBS OF PLACE.

Où, Lat. ubi, O. Fr. *u. Ailleurs,* aliórsam. *Ça,* ecce hac, and *là,* illac (already treated of on p. 113) ; their compounds, are *de ça, de là. Ici,* ecce hic (see p. 113). *Partout,* per totum ; *dont* (see p. 114) ; *loin,* longe ; *dans,* O. Fr. *dens.* In Old French *intus* became *ens,* and de-intus, *deins* or *dens,* —compound, *de dans ; en,* O. Fr. *ent,* Latin inde (see above, p. 110).

Céans, O. Fr. *caïens*, or *ca-ens*, i.e. **ecce-hac-intus.** The O. Fr. *léans* or *laiens*, **illac-intus,** was the corresponding adverb. *Alentour*, O. Fr. *à l'entour*, whence its etymology is clear enough. *Amont*, **ad montem,** i.e. 'up stream;' its opposite is *aval*, **ad vallem,** 'down stream.' The verb *avaler* used to mean 'to descend' originally; only in later times has it been limited to its present sense of swallowing down food. Some traces of the original meaning survive in Modern French, as in the phrase, 'les bateaux *avalent* le fleuve.'

For the adverbs *avant, devant, derrière, dessus, dessous, dehors*, see below, pp. 163, 164.

To these simple adverbs must be added adverbial expressions like *nulle part, là-haut, là-bas, en dedans, jusque-là*, &c., which are compounded of simple adverbs: and finally there is the adverb *environ*, compounded of *en* and the O. Fr. *viron*, a substantive derived from *virer* ('to *veer*' or 'turn round'); *environ* is therefore literally the same with *alentour*. This old word is still to be seen in the substantive *a-viron*, i. e. 'the instrument with which one turns or *veers* about.'

SECTION II.

ADVERBS OF TIME.

À présent, **ad praesentem.** *Or*, **hora** (for the suppression of *h*, see p. 81). *Maintenant* in Old French meant 'instantly' ('**manu rem tenente**'). *Hui*, **hodie,** which lingers in the legal '*d'hui* en un an.' *Aujourd'hui*, Old French, more correctly written *au jour d'hui* is a pleonasm, for it signifies literally 'on the day of this day.' *Hier*, **heri.** *Jadis*, **jamdiu.** *Fois*, O. Fr. *feis, fes, ves*, from Latin **vice** (for the change of v into *f*, see p. 59). Its compounds are, *autre-, par-, quelque-, toute-fois*. *Naguères*, O. Fr. *n'a guères*, is a compound of *avoir* and *guères*, which originally meant 'much:' 'je l'ai vu n'a guères,' i. e. ' I have seen him no long time ago.' In Old French the verb was not invariable ; in the twelfth century there were such phrases as ' la ville était assiégée, *n'avait guères,* quand elle se rendit,' i. e. ' the town had not long been besieged before it surrendered.' Remark too that the Old French has *n'a guère, n'avait guère,* where Modern French would have *n'y a guère, n'y avait guère :* the Old French not saying, *il y a,* but *il a* (illud habet), according to the rule of the objective case (see above, p. 89). Thus, ' il a un roi qui . . .' (illud habet regem), ' il n'avait aucuns arbres dans ce pays ' (illud non habebat aliquas arbores). *Roi, arbres,* are here in the objective case ; in Old French the subjective would have been *rois* (rex), &c. From the thirteenth century onwards the *y* appears in this phrase. But the old form *il a* is still to be met with in the seventeenth century, in what is commonly called the Marotic style : Racine writes—

> ' Entre Leclerc et son ami Coras
> *N'a pas longtemps,* s'émurent grands débats.'

(As to the etymology of *guères,* see below, p. 160). *Quand,* quando. *Demain,* de mane. The Latin mane gives the French substantive *main :* ' Il joue du *main au soir,*' i. e. ' from morn to eve.' De mane formed the adverb *demain,* which meant originally ' early in the morning.'

Tôt, O. Fr. *tost.* The origin of this word is obscure. By combining it with the adverbs *aussi, bien, plus, tant,* have been formed the compounds *aussi-tôt, bien-tôt, plus-tôt, tant-tôt. Longtemps* (from *long* and *temps,* Lat. longum tempus). *Toujours,* in Old French always written *tous jours,* simply a shortened form of the phrase *tous les jours.* There used to be an adverb *sempres* in Old French formed from the Latin semper, but it disappeared in the fifteenth century.

Encore, in Old French *anc ore,* from the Latin hanc horam, 'at this hour.' This was the first meaning of the word, as is seen in the following passage : ' J'ai vu Paris, et j'y retournerai *encore*, quand je reviendrai en France,' i. e. ' *at the hour* in which I return to France.'

Désormais, O. Fr. *dès ore mais* (see under the prepositions, below, p. 164, for the origin of the word *dès*). *Ore* is simply **hora**, and *mais* from **magis**, signifies 'further,' 'more ' (= *davantage*). Thus then *dès ore mais* signifies word for word, 'from this hour forwards,' or, 'from the present hour to one later,' i. e. ' dating from this present hour.'

Dorénavant, O. Fr. *d'ore en avant*, from this present time onwards, starting from this present hour [1].

Jamais. *Jà* and *mais ; jà* from **jam**, 'from this moment,' as we have seen on p. 152, and *mais* from **magis**, ' more.' These two words could be separated in Old French ; as, '*Jà* ne le ferai *mais*,' i. e. ' from this moment I will never do it again.'

Souvent, Latin **subinde**, which had the same sense in the common Latin. For the change of **inde** into *ent*, see above, p. 110.

Tandis, **tam diu**, formerly signified ' during this time.' In the thirteenth century men said, ' Le chasseur s'apprête à tirer, bande son arc ; mais la corde se rompt, et *tandis*, le lièvre s'enfuit.' As late as Corneille we have—

> ' Et *tandis*, il m'envoie
> Faire office vers vous de douleur et de joie.'

Vaugelas and Voltaire, ignorant of the historic ground for this phrase, have blamed it as incorrect. It is quite right.

Lors, O. Fr. *l'ore*, Latin **hora**, ' at this hour ;' its compound is *alors*, O. Fr. *à l'ore*.

---

[1] It may be seen hence how frequently the Latin **hora** (under the forms *ore, or*), occurs in French adverbial phrases : *or, lors* (*l'ore*), *désormais, dorénavant, encore*, &c.

Puis, depuis : see under the prepositions, p. 164.

Ensuite, en and *suite. Enfin, en* and *fin.*

Donc, tunc.

Auparavant, from *au* and *par-avant.* The article *au* was added in the fifteenth century. Old French used *par-avant :* 'Je ne voulus point être ingrat,' says Froissard, 'quand je considérai la bonté qu'il me montra *par-avant.'*

Deja, de and jam. *Tard,* tarde

Soudain, O. Fr. *soubdain,* Latin subitáneus.

Under adverbs of time may also be classed a great variety of adverbial phrases, like *tout à coup, d'ordinaire, de bonne heure, l'autre jour,* &c.

SECTION III.

ADVERBS OF MANNER.

As to the formation of these adverbs, which for the most part end in *-ment,* see above, p. 154.

To this division may be attached a whole class of adjectives, like *vrai, bon, fort, juste,* which do the work of adverbs (as in 'sentir *bon,*' 'courir *fort,*' 'dire *vrai,*' 'voir *juste,*' &c.), and answer to the neuter adjectives of the Latin (as *bene, breve, docte,* &c.). We need make no remark on this class beyond saying that they were far more numerous in Old French than now : thus, in the thirteenth century men said 'aller *lent,*' 'agir *laid,*' 'aimer *grand,*' '*faire seul,*' &c., instead of 'aller *lentement,*' 'agir *laidement,*' 'aimer *grandement,*' 'faire *seulement,*' &c.

SECTION IV.

ADVERBS OF INTENSITY.

These are twenty-five in number.

Si, sic. Its compounds are— *aussi,* O. Fr. *alsi,* Lat. aliud sic ; *ainsi,* O. Fr. *asi,* Lat. hoc sic.

Assez, adsatis, signified originally 'much,' 'very much,' and was put after the substantive. In every page of the 'Chanson de Roland,' we find such phrases as 'Je vous donnerai *or et argent assez*,' i. e. 'plenty of gold and silver' *trop assez*, 'much too much'; *plus assez*, 'much more', &c. So too the Italian *assai* is used; *presto assai* (prestus adsatis), 'very quick indeed' (but not = *assez vite*).

Tant, tantum. Its compounds are, *autant* (O. Fr. *al-tant*), aliud tantum; *atant*, ad tantum (this word, signifying 'then,' occurs as late as La Fontaine); *partant*, per tantum = 'consequently' (or 'by so much'). So La Fontaine writes—

> 'Les tourterelles se fuyaient
> Plus d'amour, *partant* plus de joie.'

Pourtant, *pour* and *tant*, This word, now a synonym to *néanmoins*, 'notwithstanding,' signified in Old French 'pour cette cause,' 'for this reason.' Montaigne speaks of a soldier who gave no quarter to his foe, and adds, '*Pour tant*, il ne combattoit que d'une masse,' meaning, 'and *for this reason* he only fought armed to the teeth.'

Ensemble. O. Fr. *ensemle*, Lat. in-simul. For the change of ml into *mbl*, see above, p. 73.

Pis, pejus.

Mieux, O. Fr. *melz*, *meilz*; Lat. mélius.

Peu from paucum, as *Eu* from Aucum; *feu* from focum; *jeu* from jocum.

Tellement, *telle* and *ment*. For *telle*, see p. 117, and for *ment*, p. 153.

Beaucoup, *beau* and *coup*. This word is, relatively speaking, new, and can be traced back only as far as to the fourteenth century. *Grand coup* was the more common phrase, but above all the adverb *moult*, multum, was employed. As to *coup* (O. Fr. *colp*), *colp* is colpus, which is met with in common Latin in the same sense: ' Si quis alterum voluerit occidere, et colpus praeter fallierit, et ei fuerit ad probatum 2000 dinarios . . . culpabilis indicetur[1].' Colpus was also written colphus, and is the Lat. colaphus, a box on the ear, blow, slap; Gr. κόλαφος. For the change from cólaphus to colphus, colpus, see p. 35.

Moins, minus. *Plus,* plus.

Bien, bene. *Mal,* male; whence *malséant, mal-veillant,* &c.

Combien, comme bien. Comme, com in Old French, is quomodo.

Comment, from *comme,* quomodo, with the suffix -*ment* already treated of.

Davantage. O. Fr. *d'avantage; de* having here the sense of ' from'; (*avantage* is from ab-ante -agium, see p. 177).

Guère. O. Fr. *gaires,* which means ' much.' In Provençal this word is spelt *gaigre,* and comes from the O. H. Germ. *weigaro,* which is in Mid. H. Germ. *weiger*[2]. This etymology is sound in its foundations. The German *w* passes into the French *g,* as in *werra, guerre,* &c., and the Provençal *gaigre* keeps the medial *g* of *weiger.*

Trop. Low Lat. troppus, from the O. H. Germ. *drupo.*

Presque, pres and *que.*

SECTION V.

ADVERBS OF AFFIRMATION AND NEGATION.

These are six in number.

Oui, O. Fr. *oïl.* In Old French the Latin pronoun hoc became *o,* the *h* disappearing as in *orge,* hordeum; *or,* hora; *avoir,* habere, &c. In the thirteenth century ' dire ni *o* ni

---

[1] *Salic Law,* xviii. 1.
[2] As in the word *unweiger* (=not much).

non' was used to express 'neither yes nor no.' The Latin compound **hoc-illud** (= 'that's the very thing') became *o-il*, the medial *c* disappearing, as it did from **plicare**, *plier ;* **jocare**, *jouer*, &c. To this *oïl*, or **hoc-illud**, corresponded the Old French *nen-il*, non-illud, which became in Modern French *nenni*, just as *oïl* has become *oui*[1].

Non, Lat. **non**.

Ne, O. Fr. *nen*, Lat. **non**.

Before we touch on the prepositions we must take notice of a number of adverbial phrases which express negation[2]. To strengthen the expression of our judgments, we are wont to join an illustration or comparison to them (thus we say 'as poor as Job,' 'as strong as a lion,' &c.), or an expression of value (as 'not worth a farthing.') So did the Latins: they would say a thing was not worth an **as**, a feather, a speck in a bean, **hilum**. Hence **ne-hilum**, and **nihil**.

> ' Nil igitur mors est, ad nos *neque* pertinet *hilum*.'
>
> (Lucr. iii. 483.)

There are six similar adverbial phrases to express a negative in French:

1. *Pas*, Lat. **passus**: 'ne point faire un *pas*.'
2. *Point*, Lat. **punctum**: ' Je ne vois *point*.'

---

[2] Some old-fashioned etymologists have tried to derive *oui* from the verb *ouïr* (**audire**), past part. *ouï;* but they have not seen, on the one side, that this past part. was always, in the middle ages, *oït* (**audítus**); and, on the other side, that *oui* was always *oïl*. To change *t* into *l* would have been a thing unheard of in the history of the language: and we may say at once that any derivation which pays no attention to the letters which are retained, changed, or thrown out, must be rejected. And, besides, the analogy between *oïl* (**hoc-illud**) and *nen-il* (**non-illud**) would by itself alone prove the truth of the derivation we have advanced—a derivation justified also by the strict rule of permutation of letters.

[2] See Schweighauser, *De la negation dans les langues romanes*, and Chevallet, iii. 330–340.

3. *Mie,* Lat. mica (which signified a speck or grain). It became *mie* just as **urtica** became *ortie;* **vesica,** *vessie;* **pica,** *pie,* &c. *Mie* was used as a negation up to the end of the sixteenth century, as ' Je ne le vois *mie*'; and the Latin **mica** had the same usage. So Martial (vii. 25) writes, ' **Nullaque mica salis.**'

4. *Goutte,* Lat. **gutta**: also used negatively in Latin, as in Plautus:

> ' Quoi neque parata gutta certi consilii.'

This phrase, which formerly was in general use (so '*ne* craindre *goutte,*' '*n*'aimer *goutte,*' &c.) has been restricted since the seventeenth century to the two verbs *voir* and *entendre :* *n*'y voir *goutte,*' '*n*'y entendre *goutte.*'

5. *Personne,* Lat. **persona,** with *ne* takes the sense of ' no one.'

Rien, Lat. **rem,** was a substantive in Old French, with its original signification of ' thing'; so ' la *riens* que j'ai vue est fort belle,' and ' une très-belle *riens.*' Joined with a negative, it signifies ' no-thing,' just as *ne* . . . *personne* signifies ' no one,' ' Je *ne* fais *rien,*' ' I am doing nothing.' This usage of *rien* is very proper, and it only abandoned its natural sense of ' thing' to take that of ' nothing' (as in the phrase ' on m'a donné cela pour *rien*'), after having been long used with *ne* to form a negative expression. This history of the word *rien* explains that passage of Molière in which it is both negative and affirmative (École des Femmes, ii. 2):

> ' Dans le siècle ou nous sommes
> On ne donne *rien* pour *rien.*'

Finally, we may observe generally that at first these adverbial phrases *pas, mie, goutte, point,* &c., were used in a substantival sense. i. e. they were always used in comparison, and had a proper value of their own: ' Je *ne* marche *pas,*' ' I do not move *a step*'; ' Je *ne* vois *point,*' ' I do not see a *bit*'; 'Je *ne* mange *mie*,' 'I do not eat *a bit*'; 'Je *ne* bois *goutte*,' 'I do not drink *a drop*'; &c., &c.

CHAPTER II.

PREPOSITIONS.

The Latin prepositions have, for the most part, survived in French: though **ab, cis, ex, ergo, ob, prae, propter,** and some others of less importance, have perished.

Such new prepositions as have been formed by the French tongue are either (1) compounds of simple prepositions, as *envers,* **in-versus**; *encontre,* **in-contra**; *dans,* **de-intus,** &c.; or (2) substantives, as *chez,* **casa**; or (3) present participles (or gerunds), as *durant, pendant, moyennant, nonobstant,* &c.

SECTION I.

PREPOSITIONS DRAWN FROM THE LATIN.

These are ten in number:

(1) *A,* **ad**; (2) *entre,* **inter**; (3) *contre,* **contra**; (4) *en,* **in,** whence *en-droit, en-vers, en-contre,* &c.; (5) *outre,* **ultra**; (6) *par,* **per**; (7) *pour,* O. Fr. *por,* Lat. **pro** (for this transposition see above, p. 77); (8) *sans,* **sine**; (9) *vers,* **versus**; (10) *sur,* O.Fr. *sour,* Lat. **super**; this form *sour* survives in *sour-cil,* **supercilium.**

SECTION II.

PREPOSITIONS FORMED FROM MORE THAN ONE LATIN PREPOSITION.

These are four in number:

1. *Avant,* **ab-ante.** **Abante** is not rare in inscriptions[1]. For the change of **b** into *v* see above, p. 60.

---

[1] We have a curious illustration of the use of this form in the old Roman grammarian Placidus. He strongly objects to this

2. *Devant,* O. Fr. *davant,* compounded of *de* and *avant*
ab-ante.

3. *Puis,* post, has for its compounds *de-puis,* and *puîné*.
the latter in O. Fr. *puis-né,* from the Lat. post-natus[1].

4. *Vers,* versus, has for a compound *en-vers.*

SECTION III.

PREPOSITIONS FORMED FROM LATIN PREPOSITIONS COMBINED WITH ADVERBS, PRONOUNS, OR ADJECTIVES.

1. *Dans,* O. Fr. *dens.* Lat. intus, which made *ens* in
Old French, became de-intus in composition, whence O. Fr.
dens, now *dans.*

2. *Derrière.* Retro, O. Fr. *rière* (as in *rière-fief,* &c.)
became in composition *arrière* and *derrière* (ad-retro and
de-retro).

3. *Sus,* Lat. susum, often used for sursum, and to be
found in Plautus, Cato, Tertullian, &c. So Augustine writes
'Jusum vis facere Deum, et te susum,' 'you wish to de
press God, and exalt yourself.' De-susum produced *dessus*
The simple *sus* survives in such phrases as 'courir *sus,*' 'er
sus,' &c.

4. *Dessous,* i. e. *de* and *sous;* *sous* comes from the Lat
subtus,

5. *Deçà, delà,* from *de çà* and *de là.*

6. *Parmi,* O. Fr. *par-mi,* from *par,* per, and *mi,* medium.

7. *Selon,* O. Fr. *sullonc, selonc,* Lat. sublongum.

8. *Dès,* Lat. de-ex.

---

vulgar word, and warns his hearers against it—'Ante me fugi
dicimus, non Ab-ante me fugit; nam praepositio praeposition
adjungitur imprudenter: quia ante et ab sunt duae praeposi·
tiones.' (*Glossae,* in Mai, iii. 431.)

[1] [Cp. *ainé,* from ante-natus.]

SECTION IV.

PREPOSITIONS WHICH ARE REALLY PARTICIPLES.

Of these the chief are *durant, pendant, suivant, touchant, nonobstant, joignant, moyennant,* &c.

In Old French the participle was often put before the noun to which it was related, in phrases in which it answered to the ablative absolute of the Latins; as in the passages 'L'esclave fut jeté au feu, *voyant le roi,*' 'in the king's presence,' **vidente rege**; 'Un des parties vient de mourir *pendant le procès,*' re pendente.[1] After the sixteenth century these inversions were no longer understood, and the French Academy, ignorant of the history of the language, treated these participles as prepositions.

1. *Durant,* from *durer.* '*Durant* le jour,' eunte die. The French Academy decreed that 'sa vie *durant*' was an inversion of the proper order of words; wrongly, for 'durant sa vie' is the real inversion.

2. *Moyennant,* pres. part. of the old verb *moyenner,* 'to give means to one': 'il échappa *moyennant* votre aide,' i. e. 'your help giving him the means of doing so.'

3. *Nonobstant,* **non obstante**; i. e. 'nothing hindering.'

4. *Pendant,* from *pendre:* '*pendant* l'affaire,' pendente re.

SECTION V.

PREPOSITIONS FORMED FROM SUBSTANTIVES.

These are seven in number:

1. *Chez.* The Latin phrase **in casa** became in Old French *en chez;* and so in the thirteenth century one would have said 'il est *en chez* Gautier' 'est **in casa** Walterii.' In the four-

---

[1] See Chevallet, iii. 335.

teenth century the preposition *en* disappears, and we find the present usage, ' il est *chez* Gautier.'

2. *Faute*, from the substantive *faute.*

3. *Vis-à-vis* (**visus-ad-visum**, 'face to face'). In Old French *vis* signified what the Modern French *visage* does, ' the face.'

4. *Malgré*, O. Fr. in two words, ' *mal gré;* from *mal,* malum, and *gré*, gratum. It is therefore equivalent to *mauvais gré.*

5, 6. *À cause de* and *à côté de* are formed by means of the substantives *cause* and *côté.*

SECTION VI.

PREPOSITIONS FORMED FROM ADJECTIVES AND ADVERBS.

1. *Hors.* See p. 66.

2. *Hormis*, O. Fr. *hors-mis,* i.e. = *mis hors.* In this Old French phrase the participle *mis* used to be declinable. Thus in the thirteenth century people said 'Cet homme a perdu tous ses enfants, *hors mise* sa fille.' In the fifteenth century the participle *mis* became inseparably fixed to the particle *hors,* and in course of time the phrase *hors-mis, hormis,* became a preposition.

3. *Rez*, Lat. **rusus.** In Old French *rez* or *ras* was equivalent to *rasé,* shorn. ' Avoir les cheveux *ras* '; ' à *ras* de terre,' i.e. on the smooth-shorn level of the ground; so ' *rez* de chaussée' is the floor of a house which is ' au *ras,*' i.e. on the level of the road.

4. *Lèz*, Lat. **latus.** In Low Latin latus was used as = **juxta,** 'near': 'Plexitium **latus** Turonem,' Plessis-*lèz*-Tours, i.e. near Tours; so Passy-*lèz*-Paris, Champigny-*lèz*-Langres. In Old French *lèz* was a substantive: 'Le roi est sur trône, et son fils à son *lèz* (at his side, **ad latus**).

5. *Jusque.* See pp. 65, 66.

6, 7. *Voici, voilà*, O. Fr. *voi-ci, voi-la ;* from the imperative of *voir* and the adverbs *ci* and *là*. Consequently separable in Old French, as in '*voi* me *là*' (now 'me *voilà*'). In the sixteenth century we still find Rabelais saying '*voy* me *ci* prêt.' The French Academy, ignorant of the meaning of this phrase, decreed that *voici, voilà* were prepositions, and therefore inseparable.

SECTION VII.

PREPOSITIONS COMPOUNDED OF THE ARTICLE AND A PREPOSITION WHICH STANDS FOR A SUBSTANTIVE.

Au dedans, au dehors, au delà, au-dessous, auprès, au-devant, au travers.

SECTION VIII.

PREPOSITIONS COMPOUNDED OF A SUBSTANTIVE OR AN ADJECTIVE, PRECEDED BY THE ARTICLE.

Au lieu, au milieu, au moyen, le long, autour, au bas, du haut, &c.

CHAPTER III.

CONJUNCTIONS.

We will take them in this order: (1) simple conjunctions, which come from Latin conjunctions, as *car*, quare, &c.; (2) conjunctions formed from Latin particles, as *aussi*, aliud sic, &c.; (3) conjunctival phrases, formed by adding the conjunction *que* to certain particles, as *tandis que, quoique,* &c.

SECTION I.

SIMPLE CONJUNCTIONS.

These are eleven in number :

1. *Car*, quare. In Old French this word retained its original sense of *pourquoi*, 'why.' In the thirteenth century men said 'Je ne sais ni *car* ni comment,' 'I know neither why nor how.'

2. *Comme*, O. Fr. *cume*, Lat. quomodo.

3. *Donc*, Lat. tunc.

4. *Et*, Lat. et.

5. *Ou*, O. Fr. *o*, Lat. aut. For the change of au into *o*, see p. 51.

6. *Quand*, Lat. quando.

7. *Que*, O. Fr. *qued*, Lat. quod.

8. *Mais*, Lat. magis : formerly bore the sense of *plus*, 'more'—a sense retained in the phrase 'je n'en peux *mais*,' 'I can do no more,' and in the old adverb *désormais*, see p. 157.

9. *Ni*, O. Fr. *ne*, Lat. nec. In Molière even we find '*ne* plus,' '*ne* moins.'

10. *Or*, Lat. hora, signified 'now' in Old French '*Or*, dîtes-moi,' &c.

11. *Si*, Lat. si. Compound *si-non*. In Old French the two particles were separable : ' Je verrai, *si* lui-même *non*, au moins son frère.'

SECTION II.

COMPOUND CONJUNCTIONS.

These are ten in number :

1. *Ainsi*, O. Fr. *asi*. Origin unknown [perhaps from ante-sic].

2. *Aussi*, O. Fr. *alsi*, Lat. aliud sic.

3. *Cependant*, from *ce* and *pendant*, literally = *pendant cela :* ' Nous nous amusons, et *ce pendant* la nuit vient.'

4. *Encore*, O. Fr. *ancore*, Lat. hanc horam (Ital. anc-ora). See p. 156.

5. *Lorsque; lors* and *que*. For *lors*, see p. 157. This word may even now be broken up, as ' *lors* même *que*.'

6. *Néanmoins*, O. Fr. *néant-moins*, from *néant* and *moins*. *Néant*, Lat. necentem * literally = *rien, non*, ' nothing.' Thus used by La Fontaine :—

Car j'ai maints chapitres vus
Qui pour *néant* se sont tenus.'

Néan-moins is equivalent to ' ne pas moins,' ' none the less':
' Il est fort jeune, et *néanmoins* sérieux,' i. e. ' none the less
for that.'

7. *Plutôt*, from *plus* and *tôt*.   See p. 156.

8. *Puisque; puis* and *que*.   See p. 164.

9. *Quoique; quoi* and *que*.   See p. 114.

10. *Toute fois*.   See p. 59.

SECTION III.

CONJUNCTIVAL PHRASES.

These are formed by the help of (1) adverbs—*tandis,
alors, sitôt, aussitôt, tant, bien, encore, afin*, followed by the
conjunction *que;* (2) prepositions—*sans, dès, jusqu'à-ce,
apres, avant*, also all followed by *que*. The etymology of these
words will be found in their proper places above.

CHAPTER IV.

INTERJECTIONS.

If we set aside such exclamations as *paix! courage!* &c.,
which are elliptical propositions, (*faites*) *paix!* (*ayez*)
courage! &c., rather than interjections properly so called,
there will remain but little to be said on this subject : for
real interjections are fundamentally common to the speech
of all nations (as *oh! ah!* &c.).   Two alone, *hélas* and
dame, have (as far as form goes) a real philological interest.

Hélas, written in Old French *hé! las!* is composed of the
interjection *hé!* and the adjective *las*, lassus (= unhappy).
In the thirteenth century we have ' Cette mère est *lasse* de la
mort de son fils.'   ' Hé! *las!* que je suis!' 'ah! *sad* that I
am!' = woe is me!   In the fifteenth century the two words

were joined together in the inseparable *hélas!* At the same time *las* lost all its primitive significance, and passed from the sense of sorrow to that of fatigue, as also happened in the cases of *gêne* and *ennui*, which at first meant ' vexation' and ' hatred.'

Dame! Lat. **Dómine-Deus**, or **Domne-Deus**, became in Old French *Dame-Dieu*, a phrase to be found perpetually in MSS. of the middle-ages: ' *Dame-Dieu* nous aide.' *Dame-Dieu*, first used as a subjective case, came afterwards to be used as an interjection, and was thence shortened into *Dame* by itself.

BOOK III.

ON THE FORMATION OF WORDS.

By the word 'affixes' we mean whatever parts of words are added to the root with a view to modifying its meaning. Thus, given the root 'form,' we produce from it the words 'in-form-ation,' 're-form-ation,' &c., where *in-*, *re-*, *-tion* are affixes ('*affixa,*' fixed on to a root). We call them *prefixes* if they are put before the root (*re-* in the word 'reform'); suffixes if they follow after it (*-tion* in the word 'reformation').

Prefixes, when joined to roots form *compound* words; suffixes form *derivatives*. We will take these in order; in other words, will review first all prefixes, and then all suffixes.

CHAPTER I.

COMPOUND WORDS.

We must distinguish between the composition (1) of nouns, (2) of adjectives, (3) of verbs, (4) of particles, the most numerous and important of all. And we must also consider the préfixes from two points—that of their origin, and that of their form.

1. As to their origin. They may be either Latin in origin, as *re-nier*, *dé-lier*, from re-negare, de-ligare; or French in origin, that is to say, created on the model of Latin prefixes, as in the case of *re-change*, but having no corresponding word from which they come.

2. As to form. Here it is especially necessary (as also in the study of derivatives) to distinguish clearly between the two classes of words which make up the French language (see above, Introduction, II, i–iv) ; namely, such compounds as *sour-cil* (**super-cilium**), or *sur-venir* (**super-venire**), which have been formed by the people; and on the other hand, such as *supér-iorité*, or *super-fétation*, which have been constructed by the learned.

SECTION I.

OF THE ACCENT ON COMPOUNDS.

In the case of nouns, adjectives, and verbs, the compound word is accented in the ordinary way, as *or-fèvre* (**auri-faber**), *aub-épine* (**alba-spina**), *main-tenir* (**manu-tenere**), because these words are so closely attached to one another that they have entirely lost their separate existence.

In treating of the composition of particles (such as the de-, re-, in deputare, reputare, *députer*, *réputer*) it is needful, if we would explain the part played by the Latin accent, to distinguish between Latin compounds which have come down into French, and compounds constructed by the French themselves.

§ 1. *Latin Compounds which have come down into French.*

'In the case of most words borrowed from the Latin, their primitive condition, as compounds has been lost sight of, and the French language has treated them as simple words. The result has been that, as the 'accent often lay on the determining or emphatic particle, the word which followed it has been destroyed or so contracted as to become utterly indistinguishable, while the particle itself has lost its original sense : so sarcóphagus came to O. Fr. *sarqueu,* Fr. *cercueil ;* trifolium, became *trèfle ;* cólloco, *couche ;* cónsuo, *couds.* But, in many words, the French language has wished to express both the force of the determining particle, and also that of the word following it. To accomplish this, in the case of words which would naturally (through the position of the accent), have lost their form, like those we have just mentioned, the accent was thrown forward a syllable, and the word following the determining syllable received it, just as if it had never been a compound at all : thus é-levo became e-lévo, whence *elève ;* ré-nego, re-négo, Fr. *renie ;* cómpater, compáter, Fr. *compère,* &c. This shifting of the accent, caused by the importance of the sense of the latter part of these compounds, took place no doubt in the time of the 'Rustic Latin,' and before the formation of French. It was a good plan for bringing out the force of simple words, which had almost perished when in composition, for words regularly formed did not retain a single trace of them[1].'

§ 2. *Compounds constructed by the French language.*

'It was natural that in these cases the second method

---

[1] G. Paris, *Accent latin,* p. 82.

of accentuation alone should be employed : no one thought
of throwing back on the determining (or emphatic) particle
the accent belonging to the word joined to it, in those cases
in which it certainly would have been thrown back had the
words been combined in the Latin. These compound words
were then formed either by uniting particles of Latin origin
to words to which they had never been joined in Latin ; or
by prefixing to Latin or French words Latin or French particles which had not been used in composition in Latin :
as *archi-duc, vi-comte* (**vice-comes**) ; *en* (from **inde**) as *en-
lève, en-fuis, en-voie*, &c. ; *sous* (from **subtus**) as *sou-lève,
sous-trais*[1], &c.'

SECTION II.

WORDS COMPOUNDED OF NOUNS.

Of compounds formed by means of nouns, there are
three classes : — I. The combination of two substantives ;
II. Of a substantive with an adjective ; III. Of a substantive
with a verb.

I. Of two substantives : such are—*oripeau*, **auri-pellem** ;
orfèvre, **auri-faber** ; *oriflamme*, **auri-flamma** ; *usufruit*, **usus-
fructus** ; *bette-rave*, **betta-rapa** ; *pierre-ponce*, **petra-pumex** ;
connétable, **comes stabuli** ; *salpêtre*, **sal petrae** ; *ban-lieu*,
banni-locus ; *mappemonde*, **mappa mundi**. So the names of
days are formed : *Lundi*, **lunae-dies** ; *Mardi*, **Martis-dies**,
&c. So also proper names : as *Port-Vendres*, **Portus-Veneris** ;
Dampierre, **Dominus Petrus** ; *Abbeville*, **Abbatis-villa** ;
Châtelherault, **Castellum Eraldi** ; *Finisterre*, **Finis-terrae** ;
Montmartre, **Mons-Martyrum** ; *Fontevrault*, **Fontem Evraldi**.

II. Compounded of a substantive and an adjective.

i. Substantive first : *banque-roule*, **banca-rupta**[2] ; *courte-

---

[1] G. Paris, *Accent latin*, p. 83.
[2] For this word see above p. 141.

pointe, culcita-puncta ; *raifort*, radix-fortis ; *vinaigre*, vinum-acre ; *rosmarin*, ros-marinus ; *république*, res-publica ; *dimanche*, dominica. We may here add the compound *embonpoint* (*en-bon-point*), to which the Old French had a corresponding *enmalpoint ;* and also certain proper names, as *Roquefort* and *Rochefort*, Rocca-fortis ; *Château-Roux*, *Forcalquier*, Forum-Calcarium ; *Vaucluse*, Vallis-Clusa, &c.

ii. Adjective first : *aubépine*, alba spina ; *bonheur*, bonum-augurium[1] ; *malheur*, malum-augurium ; *chauvesouris ; mal-aise ; bien-aise*. Also *mi*, from medius, in the following words : — *Mi-di*, media-dies ; *mi-nuit*, media-nocte ; *mi-lieu*, medius-locus ; *mi-septembre*, &c. ; *printemps*, primum-tempus ; *prud'homme*, prudens homo ; *vifargent*, vivum argentum ; *sauf-conduit*, salvum conductum ; *quintessence*, quinta essentia ; *primevère*, prima vera. Proper names : *Courbevoie*, Curva-via ; *Clermont*, Clarus-Mons ; *Chaumont*, Calvus-Mons ; *Haute-feuille*, *Haute-rive*.

III. Compounded of a substantive and a verb : *maintenir*, manu-tenere ; *colporter*, collo-portare ; *saupoudrer*, (O. Fr. *sau, sel*, remains in *saunier*, salinarius) ; *vermoulu ; bouleverser ; licou*, ligare-collem ; *fainéant*, facere necentem* , *crucifier*, cruci-ficare.

SECTION III.

WORDS COMPOUNDED OF ADJECTIVES.

I. Of two adjectives : *clair-voyant, mort-né, nouveau-né, aigre-doux, clair-obscur*, &c.

---

[1] *Bon-heur, mal-heur*, O. Fr. *bon-eür, mal-eür*. *Eür* meant 'chance,' 'presage,' and was always a dissyllable : it comes from au(g)urium, whence *aür* (twelfth century), later *eür* Those writers who have derived this *-heur* from hora are wrong, because hora could only produce (and has only produced) a monosyllable, *heure*, with a final *e* answering to the a of hora : *eür, aür* being dissyllables, and ending with a consonant, could not have come from hora.

II. Of an adjective with a verb. The Latin -ficare becomes -*fier* in French, and enters into numerous compounds, some direct from the Latin, like **puri-ficare**, *purifier ;* others, created on the same plan, but without Latin correspondents, *ramifier, ratifier, bonifier,* &c.

SECTION IV.

WORDS COMPOUNDED OF VERBS.

I. Of two verbs, or two verbal roots: *chauffer*, **cale-ficare**; *liquéfier*, **lique-ficare**; *stupéfier*, **stupe-ficare**, &c.

II. Of an adjective with a verb. See above, Sect. III. ii.

III. Of a verb and a noun. Add to the examples given above (Sect. II, III), *édifier*, **aedi-ficare**; *pacifier*, **paci-ficare**; *versifier*, **versi-ficare**, &c.

SECTION V.

WORDS MADE FROM PHRASES.

In those compound words which are really phrases, the accent lies on the last syllable (though they often have a half-accent, which is commonly neglected): *vaurien* (*vaut-rien*), *fainéant* (*fait-néant*), *couvre-chef, va-et-vient, hochequeue, licou* (*lie-cou*), *tourne-sol, vole-au-vent, passe-avant,* &c. The word *bégueule* (O. Fr. *bée-gueule*) is formed from *bée*, 'open,' past participle of the old verb *béer* or *bayer* (which survives in the phrase, '*bayer* aux corneilles'), and *gueule*, gula. *Bégueule* thus signifies 'one who keeps his mouth open'— mark of wonder and folly. The word *bée* is still used for the sluice of a water-mill.

SECTION VI.

WORDS COMPOUNDED WITH PARTICLES.

These will be taken in the following order:—1. Prepositional particles; 2. Qualitative; 3. Quantitative; 4. Negative.

§ 1. *Prepositional Particles.*

These are thirty in number:

1. **Ab**, Fr. *a, av.* This particle, which carries with it the notion of movement away, furnishes very many compounds: *avant*, ab-ante; *avorter*, ab-ortare *[1], &c.

2. **Ad**, Fr. *a, av.* In Latin ad gives to the root the sense of drawing together, and thence of augmentation: *avertir*, ad-vertere; *arriver*, ad-ripare[2], &c. New compounds are: *achever* (from *à chef*, i.e. = *à bout*, 'to the end.' In Old French the phrase ran, 'venir *à chef*,' = 'venir *à bout*'), *accoucher, abaisser, avérer, affût* (from *à* and *fût*, Latin fustis), *appât, affaire (à faire)*, &c.

3. **Ante**, Fr. *ans, ains.* The Latin ante-natus became *ains-né* in the French of the twelfth century, *ais-né* in the fifteenth, *aîné* in the seventeenth. The corresponding word is post.natus, O. Fr. *puis-né*, now *puiné*[3].

The compound ab-ante, Fr. *avant*, acts as prefix to very many words; as *avant-bras, avant-scène, avant-garde*, &c. See above, p. 163.

4. **'Αντί**, Fr. *anti.* This prefix, which must not be confounded with ante, indicates opposition[4], as *antipode, antipathie, antichrist*.

5. **Cum**, Fr. *co, com, con.* *Cailler* (O. Fr. *coaillier*), coagulare (see above, p. 71); *couvrir*, co-operire; *correspondre*, con-respondere. New compounds are *complot, compagnon*

---

[1] Learned words are *ab-juration, ab-ject, ab-latif*, &c.
[2] Learned words are *ad-judication, ad-ministration, ad-orer*, &c.
[3] Learned words are *anté-diluvien, anti-dater, anti-ciper*, &c.
[4] We pass by the modern prefixes of technical words derived from Greek, such as *ana-*, ἀνά, as in *ana-logie*; *épi-*, ἐπί, as in *épi-graphie*; *hyper-*, ὑπέρ, as in *hyper-trophie*. Their etymology offers no difficulties or peculiarities. 'Αντί stands in the text (although it has no right there, being solely a learned prefix), that there may be no confusion between it and ante.

(from **cum** and **panis**, ' who eats bread with one '). The Low Latin word was, in the nominative, **companio**, whence O. Fr. *compain ;* and in the accusative, **companionem**, Fr. *compagnon.*

6. **Contra**, Fr. *contre. Contreseing*, **contra-signum**; *contre-poids, contre-faire, contre-bande, contrôle* = *contre-rôle* [1].

7. **De**, Fr. *de, dé. Déchoir, déclarer, demander, devenir, degré, délaisser, dessiner,* &c.

8. **Dis, di**, Fr. *dé, dés. Déluge*, diluvium; *dépendre*, **dis-pendere**; *déplaire*, **displacere** [2]. New compounds are *dés-agréable, dés-honneur,* &c.

9. **E, ex**, Fr. *e, es. Essoufler*, **ex-sufflare**; *essuyer*, **ex-succare**; *essaim*, **ex-amen** [3], &c. New compounds are *effacer, ébahir, échapper,* &c.

10. **Foris, foras**, Fr. *for, four. Forfait*, **foris-factum**; *fourvoyer*, **foris-viare**. Foris having produced *hors*, **foris-missum** became *hormis* (*hors-mis*). See above, p. 66.

11. **In**, Fr. *en, em. Ensemble*, O. Fr. *ensemle*, Latin **in-simul**; *enfler*, **in-flare**; *encourir*, **in-currere**; *emplir*, **im-plere**; *empreindre*, **im-primere**. New compounds are *en-gager, enrichir, embusquer, empirer* [4], &c.

12. **Inde**, Fr. *en, em. Envoyer*, O. Fr. *entvoyer*, Latin **inde-viare**. For the change from **inde** to *ent*, see above, p. 111.

13. **Inter**, Fr. *entre. Entre-voir, entre-sol, entre-tien* [5], &c.

14. **Per**, Fr. *par. Parfait*, **perfectus**; *parvenir*, **per-venire**; *parmi*, **permedium**. New compounds are *par-fumer, pardonner,* &c.

The Latins used the particle **per** to mark the highest

---

[1] Learned words are *contra-diction,* &c.
[2] Learned words are *dis-cerner, dis-crédit,* &c.
[3] Learned words are *ex-cursion, ex-ténuer,* &c.
[4] Learned words are *in-cursion, in-time,* &c.
[5] Learned words are *inter-préter, inter-venir,* &c.

degree of intensity : per-horridus, per-gratus, per-gracilis, &c.   So in French, *par-achever, par-faire*[1], &c.

15. **Post**, Fr. *puis*.   *Puíné*, · O. Fr. *puis-né*, Latin post-natus.   (See above, No. 3, **Ante**.)   Such words as *post-dater, post-hume*, &c., are modern.

16. **Prae**, Fr. *pré*.   *Précher*, **praedicare** ; *prévoir, pré-server, prétendre*, &c.

17. **Pro**, Fr. *por, pour*.   *Pour-suivre, pour-chasser, por-trait*, pro-tractus.

18. **Re**, Fr. *ré, re, r'*.   *Réduire*, re-ducere ; *répondre, re-cueillir*, re-colligere, &c.   New compounds are *rebuter (but), rehausser (haut), rajeunir (jeune), renverser (envers), de-re-chef*, &c.

19. **Retro**, Fr. *rière*.   In Old French retro made *rière* (like **petra**, *pierre*) ; this form remains in *arrière*, ad-retro, a prefix found in such compounds as *arrière-ban, arrière-boutique, arrière-neveu*, &c.   [So too *derrière*, de-retro.]   *Rétro-actif, rétro-cession*, &c., are modern words.

20. **Se**, Fr. *sé*.   *Séduire*, seducere ; *sévrer*, separare, &c.

21. **Sub**, Fr. *se, su, sou, sous*.   *Sourire*, sub-ridere ; *se-courir*, suc-currere ; *souvenir*, sub-venire.   New compound, *séjourner (jour)*.

22. **Subtus**, Fr. *sou, sous*.   *Sous-traire*, subtus-trahere ; *sous-entendu*, subtus-intendere.   New compounds are *sous-diacre, sous-lieutenant, souterrain*.

23. **Super**, Fr. *sur, sour*.   *Survenir*, super-venire ; *sourcil*, super-cilium ; *surnommer*, super-nominare.   New com-pounds are *sur-saut, sur-humain, sur-face, sur-tout*.

The words *soubre-saut*[2], super saltum ; and *subré-cargue*,

---

[1] In Old French this particle was separable.   Thus *par sage* (=*très sage*) might be written in two parts, as 'tant *par* est *sage*' (='tant il est *parsage*').   Similarly one may still say 'C'est *par* trop *fort*.'

[2] Our 'summerset.'

super-carrica (the proper French forms are *sursaut*, and *surcharge*), are of Spanish origin.

24. **Trans**, Fr. *tré, tra. Traverser*, **transversare**; *traduire*, **trans-ducere**; &c. New compounds are *trépas*, **trans-passus**; *tressaillir*, **trans-salire**[1], &c.

25. **Ultra**, Fr. *outre. Outre-passer, outre-cuidance, outre-mer*, &c. Such words as *ultra-montain*, &c., are modern.

26. **Vice**, Fr. *vi. Vicomte*, **vice-comitem**; *vidame*, **vice-dominus**. Modern words are *vice-roi, vice-consul*, &c.

§ 2. *Qualitative Particles.*

These are four in number:

1. **Bene**, Fr. *bien. Bien-fait*, **bene-factum**; *bien-heureux, bien-venu*, &c.

2. **Male**, Fr. *mal, mau. Mal-mener*, **male-minare**; *mal-traiter*, **male-tractare**; *mau-dire*, **male-dicere**; *maussade*, **male-sapidus**[2]; *malade*, **male-aptus** (see above, p. 76); *malsain*, **male-sanus**.

3. **Minus**, Fr. *mes, mé. Médire, méfaire, méprendre, méfier, mésestimer*[3], &c.

4. **Magis**, Fr. *mais*. From this word the conjunction *mais* is derived, though the French *plus* has taken the proper sense of the Latin **magis**: the old use remains in the one phrase ' n'en pouvoir *mais*.'

---

[1] Modern words : *trans-cription, trans-port*, &c.

[2] **Sápidus**, O. Fr. *sade;* whence **male-sápidus**, *maussade*.

[3] This prefix *més, mé*, does not come from the German *miss*, as has been thought, but from the Latin **minus**—an etymology confirmed by the old form of the French prefix, as well as by its form in the other Romance languages. Thus the Latin **minus-pretiare** becomes *menos-preciar* in Spanish, *menos-prezar* in Portuguese, *mens-prezar* in Provençal, and *mes-priser* or *mé-priser* in French.

§ 3. *Quantitative Particles.*

1. **Bis**, Fr. *bé, bi.* *Bévue*, whose proper sense is = *double-vue.* Learned words, compounded with *bis*, keep the Latin form. So *biscuit*, bis-coctus ; *bis-aïeul*, bis-aviolus ; *bis-cornu*, bis-cornu, &c.

2. **Medius**, Fr. *mi.* *Mi-di*, media-die ; *mi-nuit*, media-nocte ; *mi-lieu*, medio-loco ; *mi-janvier*, *mi-carême*, &c. From dimidium we get *demi ;* so *parmi*, per medium.

§ 4. *Negative Particles.*

1. **Non**, Fr. *non.* *Non-pareil*, *non-chaloir* (whose present particle exists, *nonchalant*—a compound of *chaloir*, which has been discussed above, p. 147).

2. **In**, Fr. *en.* *En-fant*, in-fantem. The learned form is *in ; in-utile, in-décis.*

CHAPTER II.

ON SUFFIXES OR TERMINATIONS.

Suffixes, like prefixes, ought to be considered in their *origin* and their *form.*

1. As to their origin. They may be either (1) of Latin origin, as *prem-ier* from **prim-arius**; (2) of French origin, that is, built on the lines of the Latin suffixes (as *encr-ier* from French *encre*), but having no corresponding Latin words.

2. As to form. We must carefully distinguish between suffixes formed by the learned, and those formed by the people : between such as *prim-aire, sécul-aire, scol-aire,* which are of the former kind, and such as *prem-ier*, prim-arius ; *sécul-ier*, saecul-aris ; *écol-ier*, schol-aris, which are of the latter description.

SECTION I.

OF THE ACCENTUATION OF DERIVED WORDS.

Latin suffixes may be classed under two heads: the accentuated, as **mort-álīs**, **hùm-ánus**, **vulg-aris**, &c.; and the unaccented or atonics, as **ás-inus**, **pórt-icus**, **mób-ilis**.

The accented Latin suffixes are retained in the French, as *mort-el, hum-ain, vulg-aire*. These suffixes (*el, ain, aire*) are further employed in French to produce fresh derived words, by attaching them to words which were without them in Latin: thus have been formed such words as *visu-el, loint-ain, visionn-aire*, derivatives constructed for the first time by the French language.

Atonic Latin suffixes, like **ás-inus**, **pórt-icus**, **júd-icem**, are all shortened as they pass into the French language[1], following therein the natural law of accent (as explained above, p. 69). So **as-inus** produced *âne;* port-icus, *porche;* jud-icem, *juge*. Consequently no subsequent derivatives could be formed from these weak suffixes: it was not till a later period that the learned, ignorant of the part played by the Latin accent in forming French terminations, foolishly copied the Latin form, but gave it a false accent, displacing it from its proper syllable. Then came up such words as *portique*, porticus; *mobile*, mobilis; *fragile*, fragilis[2]; words formed in opposition to the genius of the French language, barbarous words, neither Latin nor French, which violate the laws of accentuation of both.

---

[1] By the French language must be understood the collection of all words of unconscious and popular formation, as opposed to learned words introduced consciously into the language.

[2] Old French, which always observed the law of the accent, said, *porche*, pórticus; *meuble*, móbilis; *frêle*, frágilis; instead of *portique, mobile, fragile*.

French suffixes are to be distinguished into *nominal* (sub-stantives and adjectives) and *verbal*. In each of these classes we will study successively the suffixes which are accented in Latin, and those which are not; carefully and rigidly exclud-ing every word which has crept into the language since its proper formation.

SECTION II.

NOMINAL SUFFIXES.

§ 1. *Suffixes accented in Latin.*

Alis, Fr. *el, al. Mort-el,* mort-alis; *chept-el,* capit-ale; *hôt-el,* hospit-ale; *roy-al,* reg-alis; *loy-al,* leg-alis[1].

Amen, Fr. *aim, ain, en. Air-ain,* aer-amen; *lev-ain,* lev-amen; *ess-aim,* ex-amen; *li-en,* lig-amen.

I-men. No word with this termination has entered into French.

U-men, Fr. *on. Bét-on,* bit-umen[2].

Antia, Fr. *ance. Répugn-ance,* repugn-antia. French derivatives[3], *nu-ance, sé-ance,* &c.

Andus, endus, Fr. *ande, ende, Vi-ande,* viv-énda; *prov-ende,* provid-enda; *leg-ende,* leg-enda. French derivatives, *offr-ande, reprim-ande, jur-ande,* &c.

Antem, Fr. *ant, and; entem,* Fr. *ent. March-and,* merc-ántem; *am-ant,* am-antem. *Méch-ant* (O. Fr. *meschéant,* par-ticiple of the verb *mescheoir,* see above, p. 148) comes

---

[1] The learned language has kept *al* for this suffix; as in *hôpit-al, nat-al, capit-al.*

[2] Learned forms are -*amen, ex-amen;* -imen into -*ime, rég-ime,* reg-imen; *cr-ime,* cr-imen; -umen into *ume; bit-ume,* bit-umen; *leg-ume,* leg-umen; *vol-ume,* vol-umen.

[3] By 'French derivatives' are meant derivatives which are formed first-hand by the French language, and have no words corresponding to them in Latin.

from *més* = minus (see p. 180), and the verb *chéoir*, cadere :
thus *méchant* represents the Latin minus-cadéntem; *sergent*, servi-éntem ; *éché-ant*, ex-cad-éntem.

Anus, Fr. *ain.*   *Aub-ain,* alb-ánus; *cert-ain,* cert-ánus* ;
rom-ain, rom-ánus; *hum-ain,* hum-anus.   Anus becomes
en, ien, after a vowel, or when the medial consonant falls
out; as *chrét-ien,* christ-ianus; *anc-ien,* anc-ianus* ; *païen,*
pa[g]-anus ;   *doy-en,* de[c]-anus.   French derivatives are,
hautain, haut; chapelain, chapelle, &c.[1]

Enus, ena, Fr. *ein, in, oin, ene.   Ven-in,* ven-enum; *avoine,* av-ena; *ch-aîne* (O.Fr. *chaêne*), cat-ena.

Ardus, Fr. *ard.*   The German suffix *-hart,* Low Lat.
-ardus, which indicates intensity, has furnished the French
language with a very considerable number of derivatives,
as *pleur-ard, fuy-ard, bât-ard,* &c.

Aris, arius, Fr. *er, ier.   Prem-ier,* prim-arius; *sécul-ier,*
saecul-aris; *gren-ier,* gran-arium; *écuy-er,* scut-arius; *riv-
ière,* rip-aria; *écol-ier,* schol-aris; *sangl-ier,* singul-aris, sc.
porcus ; *fum-ier,* fim-arium.   New derivatives, *plen-ier*
(*plein*) ; *barr-ière* (*barre*), &c.[2]

The suffix *-ier,* perhaps the most fertile in the language,
has formed a number of derivatives which had no existence
in Latin.   It most frequently designates (1) names of trades,
as *boutiqu-ier, pot-ier, batel-ier, vigu-ier,* &c.; (2) objects in
daily use, as *sabl-ier, encr-ier, fo-yer,* &c.; and (3) names
of trees, as *poir-ier, pomm-ier, peupl-ier, laur-ier, figu-ier,*
&c.

Atus, Fr. *é*; ata, Fr. *ée.   Aim-é,* am-átus; *avou-é,* ad-

---

[1] Learned form, *-an: pl-an,* pl-anus; *vétér-an,* veter-anus;
&c.   As to such words as *courtis-an,* &c., they come from the
Italian (*cortigiano,* &c.), and date from the sixteenth century.
[2] Learned form, *-aire: scol-aire,* schol-aris; *sécul-aire,* saecul-
aris; *calc-aire,* calcarium.

voc-atus; *duch-é,* duc-atus; *évêch-é,* episcop-atus; *chevauch-ée,* caballic-ata; *aim-ée,* am-ata, &c.

Certain derivatives in *-ade,* as *estrap-ade, cavalc-ade, estrade, estac-ade,* &c., come from the Italian. The French form would naturally have been *-ée,* as is seen in *cavalcade* and *chevauch-ée ; estrade* and *estr-ée,* strata; *escapade* (It. *scappata*), and *échappée*[1].

Aster, Fr. *âtre.* This suffix, which gives to the root the further sense of depreciation, has produced numerous French derivatives unknown to the Latin, as *bell-âtre, douce-âtre, gentilâtre, opini-âtre, mar-âtre, par-âtre,* &c.

Acem, Fr. *ai. Vr-ai,* veracem; *ni-ais,* nidacem, &c. The learned form is *-ace: ten-ace, rap-ace, viv-ace,* &c.

Ela, Fr. *elle. Chand-elle,* cand-ela; *quer-elle,* quer-ela; *tut-elle,* tut-ela, &c.

Elis, Fr. *el, al. Cru-el,* crud-elis; *fé-al,* fid-elis.

Ellus, Fr. *el, eau. Jum-eau,* gem-ellus; *b-eau,* b-ellus, &c.

Ensis, Fr. *ois, ais, is.* Such Latin derivatives as forensis, hortensis, nemorensis, have given no words to the French, which has used this termination only for words of modern formation, such as *court-ois, bourg-eois, mat-ois, harn-ois, marqu-is,* &c.; or for proper names, as *Orléan-ais,* Aurelianensis, *Carthagin-ois,* Carthagini-ensis, &c.

Ecem, from ex, Fr. *is. Breb-is,* verv-ecem.

Icem, Fr. *is, ix, isse. Perdr-ix,* perd-ícem; *gén-isse,* jun-ícem.

Estus, Fr. *éte. Honn-éte,* hon-estus, &c.

Ista, Fr. *iste.* A suffix very common in French: *drogu-iste, ébén-iste,* &c.

Erna, Fr. *erne. Cit-erne,* cist-erna; *lant-erne,* lant-erna; *tav-erne,* tab-erna.

---

[1] Learned form, *-at: avoc-at,* avoc-atus; *consul-at,* consul-atus; *épiscop-at,* &c.

Etum, Fr. *ay, aie.* Derivatives with this termination in Latin indicated a place, or district, planted with trees. Though masc. in Latin, they became fem. in French: *aun-aie*, aln-étum; *orm-aie*, ulm-étum; *sauss-aie*, salic-étum. Hence such proper names as *Chaten-ay*, **Casten-étum**; *Rouvr-ay*, **Robor-étum**; *Auln-ay*, **Aln-étum**, &c. French derivatives are *chén-aie* (*chéne*); *houss-aie* (*houx*); *chataigner-aie* (*chátaignier*); *roser-aie* (*rosier*), &c.

Ilis, Fr. *il.* *Puer-il*, *gent-il*, &c. The suffix -īlis is joined only to nouns and adverbs; ĭlis only to verbs.

Ignus, Fr. *in, ain.* *Bén-in*, ben-ignus; *mal-in*, mal-ignus; *déd-ain*, disd-ignum, &c.

Inus, Fr. *in.* *Dev-in*, div-ínus; *péler-in*, peregr-ínus; *vois-in*, vic-ínus, &c. French derivatives are *mut-in*, *bad-in*, *cristall-in*.

Issa, Fr. *esse.* *Abb-esse*, abbat-issa; *prophét-esse*, prophet-issá; *venger-esse*, *traitr-esse*, &c.

Ivus, Fr. *if.* *Chét-if*, capt-ivus; *na-if*, nat-ivus. French derivatives are many, *pens-if*, *hát-if*, *craint-if*, *ois-if*, &c.

Lentus, Fr. *lent, lant.* *Vio-lent*, vio-léntus; *sang-lant*, &c.

Mentum, Fr. *ment.* *Véte-ment*, vesti-méntum; *fro-ment*, fru-mentum, &c. French derivatives: *ménage-ment*, *change-ment*, &c.

Orem, Fr. *eur.* *Chant-eur*, cant-órem; *sauv-eur*, salvat-orem; *su-eur*, sud-orem; *past-eur*, past-orem; *péch-eur*, peccat-orem, &c.

Osus, Fr. *eux.* *Épin-eux*, spin-ósus; *pierr-eux*, petr-ósus; *envi-eux*, invidi-osus, &c. French derivatives, *heur-eux* (O. Fr. *heur*, see p. 175), *hid-eux*, *hont-eux*, &c.

Onem, Fr. *on.* *Charb-on*, carb-ónem; *pa-on*, pav-ónem; *larr-on*, latr-ónem, &c.

Ionem, Fr. *on.* *Soupç-on*, suspic-iónem; *pige-on*, pipi-onem; *poiss-on*, L. Lat. pisc-iónem; *moiss-on*, messi-ónem; *mais-on*, mans-ionem, &c.

Tionem, Fr. *son.*   *Rai-son,* ra-tiónem; *poi-son,* po-tió-
nem; *venai-son,* vena-tiónem; *liai-son,* liga-tiónem; *saison,* sa-tiónem; *fa-çon,* fac-tiónem; *le-çón,* lec-tiónem, &c.
The form -*tion* is of learned origin, as in the words *ra-tion,
po-tion, liga-tion, fac-tion,* &c.

Tatem, Fr. *té.*   *Ci-té,* ci-tatem[1]; *sure-té,* securi-tatem ;
pauvre-té, pauper-tatem; &c. French derivatives: *nouveau-té,
opiniatre-té,* &c.

Icus, Fr. *i;* ica, Fr. *ic.*   *Am-i,* am-icus; *ennem-i,* inim-
icus; *fourm-i,* form-ica; *ort-ie,* urt-ica; *vess-ie,* vess-ica;
m-ie, m-ica; *p-ie,* p-ica. The learned form is *ique: ant-ique,
pud-ique,* &c.

Uca, Fr. *ue.*   *Verr-ue,* verr-uca; *lait-ue,* lact-uca; *charr-ue,*
carr-uca; *fét-u,* fest-uca.

Orius, Fr. *oir.*   *Dort-oir,* dormit-órium; *press-oir,* press-
órium; *dol-oire,* dolat-orium, &c. French derivatives : *parl-
oir, abatt-oir, bruniss-oir, mâch-oire, balanç-oire.*

Undus, Fr. *ond.*   *Rond,* O. Fr. *roond,* rot-undus.

Unus, Fr. *un.*   *Je-un,* O. Fr. *jeûn,* jej-unus; *Verd-un,*
Virod-unum.

Ura, Fr. *ure.*   *Mes-ure,* mens-ura; *peint-ure,* pict-ura.
French derivatives : *froid-ure, verd-ure,* &c.

Urnus, Fr. *our.*   *F-our,* f-urnus; *j-our,* di-urnus; *aubour,* alb-urnum, &c.

Utus, Fr. *u.*   *Corn-u,* corn-utus; *chen-u,* can-utus. French
derivatives in abundance : *barb-u, jouffl-u, ventr-u, membr-u,
chevel-u,* &c.

§ 2. *Suffixes which are Atonic in Latin.*

'All these suffixes disappear in the French, and are
consequently useless for the purpose of producing new

---

[1] Common Latin for civi-tatem.

derivatives ; they have however recovered their place from the time that men utterly lost sight of the genius of the language, and became ignorant of the rule of accent[1].' Thus people began to use such words as *portíque, fragíle, rigíde,* instead of *porche, frêle, roide,* from **pórtĭcus, frágĭlis, rígĭdus.**

In considering these Latin atonic suffixes we are bound strictly to reject every word that has been introduced into the French language since the period of its natural formation.

Eus, ius, Fr. *ge, che.* *Etran-ge,* **extrán-eus** ; *lan-ge,* **lán-eus** ; *delu-ge,* **diluv-ium** ; *lin-ge,* **lín-eus** ; *pro-che,* **próp-ius** ; *sa-ge,* **sáp-ius** ; *sin-ge,* **sím-ius** ; *or-ge,* **hórd-eum** ; *rou-ge,* **rúb-eus** ; *au-ge,* **alv-ea** ; *son-ge,* **somn-ium** ; *Liè-ge,* **Leod-ium** ; *Maubeu-ge,* **Malbód-ium** ; *cier-ge,* **cér-eus**[2]. For the change of **eus, ius** into *ge, che,* see above, p. 66.

Ea, Fr. *ge, gne.* `Ca-ge,* **cáv-ea** ; *gran-ge,* **grán-ea** ; *vi-gne,* **vín-ea** ; *li-gne,* **lin-ea** ; *tei-gne,* **tin-ea.** For the change of **ea** into *ge,* see above, p. 66.

Ia, Fr. *ge, che, ce* ; or it disappears altogether. *Vendan-ge,* **vindém-ia** ; *angois-se,* **angúst-ia** ; *cigo-gne,* **cicon-ia** ; *ti-ge,* **tíb-ia** ; *sè-che,* **sép-ia** ; *sau-ge,* **sálv-ia** ; *env-ie,* **invíd-ia** ; *grâ-ce,* **grat-ia** ; *histoi-re,* **histór-ia** ; *Bourgo-gne,* **Burgúnd-ia** ; *France,* **Fránc-ia** ; *Grè-ce,* **Graéc-ia** ; *Breta-gne,* **Británn-ia**[3]. For the change of **ia** into *ge,* see above, p. 65.

It-ia, Fr. *esse.* *Just-esse,* **just-ítia** ; *moll-esse,* **moll-ítia** ; *par-esse,* **pigr-ítia** ; *trist-esse,* **trist-ítia.** French derivatives : *ivr-esse, polit-esse, tendr-ésse.*

---

[1] G. Paris, *Accent latin,* p. 92.

[2] Learned form *é,* as *ign-é,* **ign-eus.**

[3] Learned form *ie,* as *chim-ie, philosoph-ie, symphon-ie, Austral-ie.* But we must not confound this termination with the proper French derivatives in *ie,* as *felon-ie (felon), tromper-ie (tromper),* &c., which are popular and very numerous.

Icem (from **ex, ix,** represented in French only by *ce, se, ge*): *her-se,* hérp-icem ; *pu-ce,* pul-icem ; *ju-ge,* jud-icem ; *pou-ce,* poll-icem ; *pon-ce,* púm-icem ; *écor-ce,* córt-icem[1].

Icus, a, um, Fr. *che, ge. Por-che,* pórt-icus ; *man-che,* mán-ica ; *ser-ge,* sér-ica ; *diman-che,* domin-ica ; *Sainton-ge,* Santón-ica ; *for-ge* (O. Fr. *faur-ge*), fábr-ica (see p. 76) ; *per-che,* pért-ica ; *piè-ge,* péd-ica[2].

Aticus is a suffix formed with **icus,** Fr. *age. Voy-age* (O. Fr. *viat-ge*), vi-áticum ; *from-age,* form-áticum ; *vol-age,* vol-áticum; *ombr-age,* umbr-áticum; *ram-age,* ram-áticum; *mess-age,* miss-áticum ; *sauv-age,* silv-áticus[3].

Hence come French derivatives: *mesur-age, labour-age, alli-age, arros-age,* &c. It has been said that these words come from a Low Latin suffix in -**agium** (as *message* from **mess-agium,** *hom-age* from **hom-agium**). But though **mess-agium** certainly exists, it is far from being the parent of the Fr. *message ;* on the contrary, it is nothing but the Fr. *message* latinised by the clergy, at a time when no one knew either the origin of the word (**missaticum**) or the nature of the suffix which formed it.

Idus disappears in French. *Pâle,* páll-idus ; *net,* nít-idus ; *chaud,* cál-idus (Low Lat. **cal-dus**) ; *tiède,* tép-idus ; *roide,* ríg-idus ; *sade,* sáp-idus ; whence *maussade,* male sap-idus[4]. See p. 180.

---

[1] Learned form *ice: cal-ice,* cál-icem.

[2] Learned form *ique: port-ique,* pórt-icus ; *fabr-ique,* fábr-ica ; *viat-ique,* viát-icum.

[3] Silva in Old French became *selve, sauve,* which, as a common noun, is lost, but survives in certain names of places, as *sauve-Saint-Benoit,* silva-S.-Benedicti. From silva came **silváticus,** whence *sauv-age,* O. Fr. *selvátge.* Nothing but a complete misunderstanding or ignorance of the laws of the formation of the French language could have ever allowed people to derive *sauvage* from **solívagus.** This word could only have produced in French the form *seulige.*

[4] Learned form *ide: rig-ide,* ríg-idus; *sap-ide,* sáp-idus; *ar-ide* ár-idus ; &c.

-Ilis, Fr. *le.* *Humb-le,* húm-ilis; *faib-le,* fléb-ilis (O. Fr. *floible); douil-le,* dúct-ilis; *meub-le,* mób-ilis; *frèle,* frág-ilis; *grê-le,* grác-ilis[1].

Inus disappears in French. *Page,* página; *jaune,* gálb-inus; *femme,* fém-ina; *frêne,* frax-inus; *dame,* dom-ina; *charme,* carp-inus; *coffre,* coph-inus[2].

Itus, Fr. *te.* *Ven-te,* vénd-ita; *ren-te,* rédd-ita; *det-te,* déb-ita; *per-te,* pérd-ita; *quê-te,* quaés-ita.

Olus, Fr. *le.* *Diab-le,* diáb-olus; *apôtre* (O. Fr. *apost-le*), apóst-olus.

The compound suffixes iolus, eolus, dissyllabic (ĭŏ, eŏ) in Latin, were contracted into a long penultimate in the seventh century, ĭō, eō, thenceforwards accented iólus, eólus, whence came the French terminations *ieul, euil, iol*: thus *fill-eul,* fil-íolus; *chevr-euil,* capr-éolus; *linc-eul,* lint-éolum; *gla-ïeul,* glad-íolus; *rossig-nol,* luscin-íolus; *aïeul,* av-íolus.

Ulus, Fr. *le.* *Tab-le,* táb-ula; *fab-le,* fáb-ula; *amb-le,* ámb-ula; *peup-le,* póp-ulus; *hièb-le,* éb-ulum; *seil-le,* sít-ula; *sang-le,* cíng-ulum; *ong-le,* ung-ula; *chapit-re,* capit-ulum[3]; *mer-le,* mér-ula; *éping-le,* spín-ula; *ensoup-le,* in-súb-ulum.

The following suffixes are formed from ulus:—

1. Ac-ulus, Fr. *ail.* *Gouvern-ail,* gubern-áculum; *ten-aille,* ten-áculum; *soupir-ail,* suspir-áculum. French derivatives: *trav-ail, ferm-ail, éventail,* &c.

2. Ec-ulus, Fr. *il.* *Goup-il,* vulp-écula. In Old French this word meant a fox, and survives still in the diminutive *goupillon,* a sprinkler, originally made of a fox's tail.

---

[1] Learned form *ile*: *mob-ile,* mob-ilis; *duct-ile,* duct-ilis; *fragile,* fragilis; &c.

[2] Learned form *ine*: *machine,* máchina, &c.

[3] Learned form *ule*: *tell-ule,* cell-ula; *calcul,* calc-ulus; *fun-amb-ule,* funamb-ulus.

3. Ic-ulus, Fr. *eil.* *Ab-eille*, ap-ícula ; *ort-eil* (O. Fr. *art-eil*), art-ículum ; *somm-eil*, somn-ículus* ; *sol-eil*, sol-ículus* ; *or-eille*, aur-ícula ; *corn-eille*, corn-ícula ; *ou-aille*, ov-ícula ; *verm-eil*, verm-ículus ; *aig-uille*, ac-ícula.

4. Uc-ulus, Fr. *ouil.* *Fen-ouil*, fen-ículum ; *gren-ouille*, ran-úcula ; *verr-ou* (O. Fr. *verr-ouil*, surviving in *verrouiller*), ver-úculum ; *gen-ou* (O.Fr. *gen-ouil*, surviving in *agenouiller*), gen-úculum.

We have seen above (p. 69) that vowels which follow the tonic syllable disappear in French; consequently the learned forms of atonic suffixes, such as *fragile*, *mobile*, &c., from fróg-ilis, mób-ilis, &c., are incorrect, seeing that they all retain the vowels after the tonic syllable, and in fact displace the Latin accent. One may indeed lay it down as a general rule that, *in the case of Latin atonic suffixes, all French words of learned origin break the law of Latin accentuation.*

SECTION III.

VERBAL SUFFIXES.

§ 1. *Suffixes accented in Latin.*

Asco, Fr. *ais;* **esco,** Fr. *ois;* **isco,** Fr. *is.* *N-ais,* n-asco[1]; *p-ais,* p-asco ; *par-ais,* par-esco ; *cr-ois,* cr-esco ; &c.

Ascere, Fr. *aître,* O. Fr. *aistre.* *N-aître,* n-áscere ; *p-aître,* p-áscere.

Ico, igo, Fr. *ie.* *L-ie,* l-igo ; *chát-ie,* cast-igo ; *n-ie,* n-ego ; &c.

Illo, Fr. *èle.* *Chanc-èle, gromm-èle, harc-èle,* &c.

Are. Fr. *er.* *Pes-er,* pens-are ; *chant-er,* cant-are ; &c.

---

[1] We have seen (p. 119) that all deponent verbs became active in form in the Low Latin.

Tiare, Fr. *cer, ser.* These are forms peculiar to the common Latin : *tra-cer,* **trac-tiare** ; *su-cer,* **suc-tiare** , *chasser,* **cap-tiare.**

§ 2. *Atonic suffixes.*

Ico, Fr. *che, ge. Ju-ge,* júd-ico ; *má-che,* mást-ico ; *ven-ge,* vénd-ico ; *ron-ge,* rúm-igo , *char-ge,* cárr-ico ; &c.   The learned form is *ique* : *revend-ique,* revénd-ico ; *mast-ique,* mást-ico.

Ere, Fr. *re. Sourd-re,* súrg-ere; *moud-re,* mól-ere; *tord-re,* tórqu-ere ; *ard-re,* árd-ere. This Old French verb, which signified ' to burn' (*brûler*), remains in the participle *ardent,* and substantive *ardeur.*

Io disappears in French. *Dépouille,* despolio.

Ulo, Fr. *le. Mou-le,* mód-ulo; *comb-le,* cúm-ulo ; *tremb-le,* trém-ulo ; *troub-le,* túrb-ulo.

Under **ulo** we may put :—

1. **Ac-ulo**, Fr. *aille,* as in *tir-aille, cri-aille,* &c.

2. **I-culo**, Fr. *ille. Fou-illé,* fod-ículo ; *saut-ille, tort-ille,* &c.

3. **U-culo**, Fr. *ouille. Chat-ouille, bred-ouille, barb-ouille,* &c.

SECTION IV.

DIMINUTIVES.

These are sixteen in number.

Aceus, Fr. *ace, asse. Vill-ace, grim-ace* (*grimer*), *popul-ace, paper-asse,* &c.

Iceus, Fr. *isse, iche. Coul-isse* (*couler*), *pel-isse* (*peau*), *can-iche.*

Oceus, Fr. *oche. Epin-oché, pi-oche.*

Uceus, Fr. *uche. Pel-uche, guen-uche.*

Aculus. See above, p. 190.

Aldus (from the Germ. *walt,* Low Lat. **oaldus,** then

aldus), Fr. *aud.* *Bad-aud, crap-aud, rouge-aud, lourd-aud, levr-aut.*

Alia, Fr. *aille.* *Bét-ail,* **besti-alia** ; *poitr-ail,* **pector-alia** ; *merv-eille,* **mirab-ilia** ; *port-ail,* **port-alia** ; *can-aille, mur-aille, bat-aille,* &c.

Ardus (from the Germ. *hart,* Low Lat. **ardus**), Fr. *ard. Bav-ard, bât-ard, fuy-ard, mign-ard, can-ard.* See above, p. 184.

Aster, Fr. *âtre.* See above, p. 185.

At, et, ot. (1) **At:** *aigl-at, louv-at, verr-at.* (2) **Et, ette:** *sach-et (sac), coch-et (coq), moll-et (mol), maisonn-ette, alou-ette,* for which see above, p. 5. (3) **Ot, otte:** *billot (bille), cach-ot (cache), brul-ot (brûle), il-ot, (île),* &c.

Ellus, illus, Fr. *eau, el, elle.* *Agn-eau,* **agn-éllus** ; *jum-eau,* **gem-éllus** ; *ann-eau,* **ann-éllus** ; *écu-elle,* **scut-élla** ; *vaiss-eau,* **vasc-éllus** ; *ois-eau,* **avic-éllus.**

Onem, ionem. See above, p. 280.

Ulus. See above, p. 285.

APPENDIX

Etymology, which enquires into the origin of words, and the laws of transformation applicable to languages, is a new science. It is only during the last thirty years that it has entered into the cycle of the sciences of observation; but the services it has rendered have won for it a rank among historical sciences, which it ought never to lose.

Before attaining its present precision, etymology, like every other science,—perhaps even more than any other,—passed through a long period of infancy, groping its way with uncertain efforts; possessing, as its stock-in-trade, only a few arbitrary resemblances, superficial analogies, and guesses at combinations.

'It is hard to realise to oneself how arbitrary was the spirit in which men sought for etymologies, so long as it consisted in placing words together at hap-hazard simply because they were like one another.

'The dreams of Plato in his "Cratylus," the absurd etymologies of Varro and Quinctilian, the philological fancies of Ménage in the seventeenth century, are matters of notoriety. Thus, for example, no one felt any difficulty in connecting *jeûne*, "fasting," with *jeune*, "young," under the pretext that *youth* is the morning of life, and one is *fasting*, when one rises in the morning! But the common course was to derive from one another two words of totally different forms, and to fill up the gulf between them with fictitious intermediate words. Thus Ménage derived the word *rat* from the Latin **mus**: " One must have first said **mus**, then **muratus**, then **ratus**, and lastly *rat !*" Nay, they even went so far as to suppose that an object could take its name from a quality the very contrary of that which it possessed, on the ground that "affirmation suggests negation;" and thus we have the famous lucus à non lucendo, on the pretext that "once in a sacred wood one has no more light[1]." '

Finally, the illusions of etymologists became proverbial, and this branch of historical knowledge was thoroughly discredited. How then did a science, now established and important, emerge from such a mass of learned bewilderment ? The clue is the discovery and application of the *comparative method*, the true method of natural sciences. ' Comparison is the chief instrument of scientific enquiry. For science is composed of generalisations: to know is to form a group, to establish a law; consequently, to pick out whatever is general from among particular facts. But if we would compel facts to deliver up to us their inner meaning, we must place them side by side, explain them by one another, in a word, compare them.'

' Every one is acquainted with the discoveries of comparative anatomy. We know how the study of the structure of animals, and the comparison of their organs (whose infinite modifications form the differentiæ of class, order, and genus), have revealed, if we may so speak, the plan of nature, and have given us a firm foundation for our classifications [2].'

The same is true of the science of language: here, doubt-

---

[1] M. Réville, *Les ancêtres des européens.*
[2] E. Schérer, *Études d'histoire et de critique.*

less, as elsewhere, comparison is as old as observation; but there are two kinds of comparison, or rather, there are two stages of comparison, through which in due succession every mind must pass.

Of these the former stage is precipitate and superficial. It governed all natural sciences up to the end of the seventeenth century, and was content to compare and class together beings or words according to their superficial likeness. Thus the ancients put the whale and the dolphin in the class of fishes, because of their external form, their habits, and their habitat in the sea; similarly the old etymologists derived the word *paresse* from the Greek πάρεσις, because, among all the languages they knew, this Greek form was most like the French word; and so they concluded, without further proof, that it came from the Greek— an easy way indeed of satisfying oneself!

To these arbitrary processes has succeeded in our day the stage of well-considered and methodical comparison; a strict and scientific comparison, which does not stop at external resemblance or difference, but dissects objects in order to penetrate even to their very essence, and their deepest analogies.

The anatomist studies the internal structure of the whale, and instantly sees that the conformation of its organs excludes it from the class of fishes, and places it among the mammalia. And similarly, instead of only studying his word from the outside, the philologer dissects it, reduces it to its elements, i.e. its letters, observes their origin and the manner of their transformation.

By a strict application of this new method, by letting facts lead instead of trying to lead them, modern philology has been enabled to prove that language is developed according to constant laws, and follows necessary and invariable rules in its transformations.

We have set forth in this book the chief characteristics of this natural history of language. Especially with a view to etymology they furnish the student with unexpected assistance, and are, in his eyes, a precious instrument, a powerful microscope with which to observe the most delicate phenomena.

Its instruments are these : Phonetics, History, Comparison.

I. Phonetics.

In the earlier part of this book[1] we divided words into their elements, that is, into their letters, and saw that the transit of the letters from Latin to French followed a regular course, each Latin letter passing into French according to fixed rules : thus e long always becomes *oi* in French, as mē, *moi;* rēgem, *roi;* lēgem, *loi;* tē, *toi;* sē, *soi;* tēla, *toile;* vēlum, *voile,* &c.

The bearings of this discovery are apparent at once : for if we will but observe these laws of change as they affect each letter in succession, we shall find them a clue to guide our researches, and to keep us from straying into wrong paths; if the etymology does not satisfy these conditions, it is naught.

Thus then the possession in detail of the transformations of the Latin letters into French[2] is the first necessity for those who would occupy themselves with etymology. If any one finds this preparatory study too minute or uninteresting, our reply is that anatomy observes and describes muscles, nerves, and vessels most minutely in detail; and draws out a catalogue of facts which may well seem dry and tiresome; but yet just as this comparative anatomy is the basis of all physiology, so is this exact knowledge of

---

[1] See above, pp. 45–86.   [2] See above, Bk. I. pp. 66–76.

orthography the beginning of all true etymology : nothing else can give it the true character of a compact and rigorous science.

We may state this new principle thus :—*We must reject every etymology, which, when the rules of permutation have been laid down by orthography, does not account for letters retained, changed, or lost.*

By the light of this principle let us take as an example the word *laitue*, and seek for its origin. We have seen above, under 'Phonetics,' p. 50, that the French combination *it* corresponds to the Latin ct; as *fa-it* from fa-ct-us; *la-it*, la-ct-em; *tra-it*, tra-ct-us; *fru-it*, fru-ct-us; *redu-it*, re-du-ct-us.

Therefore the first part of the word *laitue* (*lait*) must answer to a Latin word lact-. What is the origin of the suffix *-ue*? Now we have seen (p. 187) that this suffix is derived from the Latin suffix -uca; as *verr-ue* from verr-uca; *charr-ue*, carr-uca, &c. Thus we arrive at the form lact-uca, which is in fact the Latin word which expresses the idea involved in *laitue*, the lettuce.

This enquiry into etymology is clearly analogous to the operations of chemical analysis. The chemist puts a substance into his crucible and reduces it to its elements, and finds again the equivalent weight : so here too the elements are the letters, and our analysis, i. e. our etymology, is liable to suspicion so long as the elements have not been discovered again after the process [1].

We may sum up by saying that etymological research is subject to two rules :—(1) No 'etymology is admissible which refuses to account for all the letters of the word it proposes to explain, without a single exception; and (2) Every etymology which assumes a change of letters ought

---

[1] M. Littré.

to have in its favour at least one example of a change quite
identical with that which it assumes; otherwise, if no such
testimony can be cited, the attempt is valueless.

II. History.

Every Latin word on its way into Modern French has
gone through two changes; it has passed from Latin into
Old French, and thence into the French of to-day: thus
festa became first *feste*, and then in course of time *feste*
became *fête*. In finding the origin of a French word we
should follow a wrong track if we speculated on it in its
present state, leaping from Modern French to Latin; we must
first enquire whether there are any intermediate forms in
Old French which may explain the transition and mark the
path followed by the Latin on its way to the present French.
And besides, these intermediate forms, by bringing us nearer
to the starting-point, help us to see that point more clearly,
and often guide us to the word we are seeking without any
further researches.

An example will best illustrate the difference in this
respect between the old and the new methods of etymology.
The old etymologists were much divided as to the origin of
the word *âme:* some only thought of the sense, and therefore declared that it came from the Latin **anima**, though
they could not explain how the transformation had taken
place; others, finding the contraction of **anima** into *âme*
far too violent a change, held that it was derived from the
Gothic *ahma*, 'breath.' The case would be still ' sub judice,'
had not modern philology intervened to solve the problem
in the natural way. Substituting the observation of facts
for the play of imagination, modern philologers have seen
that it would be absurd to talk for ever over a word in its
modern form, without taking any heed to the changes it has

undergone since the origin of the language; and so they constructed the history of the word by the study of ancient texts, and shewed that in the thirteenth century *âme* was written *anme*, in the eleventh *aneme*, in the tenth *anime*, whence we pass directly to the Latin *anima.*

If we would obtain a secure foothold, we must move step by step over the intermediate forms; so as to be able to study in its gradations the deformation of the Latin word. But even here we must distinguish between two kinds of intermediate forms,—those of the old and those of the new philological school. The former assumed at a venture some improbable word as the origin of the word under consideration; and, in order to join the two ends, imagined fictitious intermediate forms to suit their purpose. Thus, Ménage pretended that he had found the origin of the French *haricot* in *faba*; and to fill up the gulf between these words he added, 'They must have said first *faba*, then *fabaricus*, then *fabaricotus*, *aricotus*, and finally *haricot.*' Such lucubrations are like a bad dream; they justify the opinion of those who have laughed at etymology, and deserve the Chevalier d'Aceilly's epigram:

> '*Alfana*[1] vient d'equus sans doute,
> Mais il faut convenir aussi
> Qu'à venir de là jusqu'ici,
> Il a bien changé sur la route;'

for the learned made a scientific toy of what they ought to have treated as a science.

The intermediate forms, diligently sought out by modern etymology, are very different; science does not ask what men 'must have said,' but what men *did* say. There are no more fanciful forms invented, as the case required

---

[1] The name given by Ariosto to Gradasso's mare. Ménage proposed to derive it from equus.

them. French philology now limits itself to a diligent passage through old texts running back to the tenth century : then noting the birth of words and the first date of their appearance, it marks the changes in them century after century. Exact observation, which leaves no room for conjecture or invention, is a preliminary but essential part of all etymological enquiry : before analysing a French word in its actual form, we must seek to obtain as many examples as we can of the word as it appeared in Old French.

M. Littré has followed this course in his admirable *Dictionnaire historique de la langue française:* instead of inventing a series of arbitrary intermediate forms, he collects under each word a series of successive examples drawn from texts, running back to the very beginnings of the French language in the eighth century. These posts once firmly fixed, he goes on to build on them an etymology, which does not arise from the word in its present shape, but from it as it existed at the birthplace of the language.

An attentive investigation into intermediate forms is the best help, after phonetics, that philology can have.

III. COMPARISON.

While popular Latin was giving birth to the French language, it also created, as we have seen (p. 10), four sister idioms to it, formed also with astonishing regularity—the permutation of the Latin letters into Italian, Spanish, Portuguese, that is to say, what are called the Romance languages, being as regular and unchanging as into French.

Consequently, we must compare the French forms with those current in the other Romance languages ; this will be the touchstone by which to try and prove all proposed hypotheses. We have just seen (p. 199) that *laitue* answers letter for letter to the Latin **lactuca.** If this etymology is correct, it will follow that the Italian *lattuga*, and the Spanish *lechuga*, whose sense is the same, spring also from the same Latin word. And this will shew us that the Italian *tt* and the Spanish *ch* come from the Latin ct: thus ITALIAN *no-tt-e*, no-ct-em; *la-tt-e*, la-ct-em; *o-tt-o*, o-ct-o; *bisco-tt-o*, bisco-ct-us; *tra-tt-o*, tra-ct-us, &c.—whence *la-tt-uga*, from la-ct-uca;—SPANISH *no-ch-e*, no-ct-em; *le-ch-e*, la-ct-em; *o-ch-o*, o-ct-o; *bisco-ch-o*, bisco-ct-us; *tre-ch-o*, tra-ct-úm, &c.— whence *le-ch-uga* from la-ct-uca. Thus we see how the parallel relations of the Romance with the French languages strengthen our previous observations, and serve as verifying tests of our hypotheses. These parallels have another use; they often shew us the road we ought to follow;—but time and space fail us, and we cannot stay to insist on the advantages that etymology can derive from careful comparison; such details would be in their right place in a 'Manual of French Ety-mology,' but are beside the mark in this short outline of the new philological method, in which we are trying to describe the great revolution which has transferred etymology from the realms of fancy to the solid ground of a historical science.

CONCLUSION.

By shewing that words grow and have a history, and that, like plants and animals, they pass through regular transfor-mations—above all by shewing that here, as elsewhere, law reigns, and that we can lay down with certainty the rules of derivation from one language to another,—modern philolo-gers have set comparative etymology on durable founda-tions, and have made a science of what seemed condemned to be confined to the regions of imagination and individual caprice.

The older system of etymology tried to explain the origin of words *a priori*, following their apparent resemblance or difference; modern etymology applies the method of the natural sciences, and holds that words ought to explain themselves, and that, instead of inventing systems, we ought to observe facts, by the help of these instruments :—Phonetics, which give us the rules of transformation from one language to another—rules which we must follow implicitly, or pay the penalty of losing our way; History of words, which passes on by certain and definite stages to the original word we are looking for, or, at any rate, brings us nearly up to it; and lastly, Comparison, which certifies and confirms the results we have arrived at.

To the fantastic imaginations of the learned of old days was due the discredit into which etymology had formerly fallen; but by the strict application of this method and these principles, comparative etymology has risen in our time to the dignity of a science.

INDEX.

A.

A, the French, 48; the Latin, 67.

Accent, continuance of Latin, 33; grammatical, 33, 85; on vowels, 67; tonic, 84; oratorical, 86; provincial, 86; on compounds, 172.

Accusative, the Latin, retained in French, 93.

Adalhard of Corbie spoke Romance, 12.

Addition of letters, 78-80.

Adjectives, French, 102-108; used as substantives, 103; compound, 175.

Adverbs, 153-163; of place, 154; time, 155; manner, 158; intensity, 158; affirmative and negative, 160.

Adverbial phrases, 161.

Ae, the Latin, 68.

Ai, the French vowel, 52.

Ailleurs, 154.

Alauda, 5.

Aller, 149.

Alphabet, French and Latin, 46-83.

Amabam, in the Langue d'Oil dialects, 19, 137.

Amont, 155.

Analytical tendencies of modern languages, 11.

Anglo-French aristocratic words, 4.

Anomalous verbs, 148-152.

Aphaeresis, 80.

Apocope, 80, 82.

Arabic words in French, 22, 23.

Armorica, long retained Celtic speech, 4, 6.

Article, the French, 100.

Atonic syllables, 68.

Au, the French, 53, 68.

Aucun, 115.

Aujourd'bui, 155.

Auparavant, 158.

Auxiliary Verbs, 123-129.

Avaler, 155.

Avant, 163.

Avoir, 127-129.

B.

B, French, 58; Latin, 76; omission of, 82.

Bacon, Roger, on French dialects, 19.

Basque tongue, 1.

Beaucoup, 159.

Belgae, 1.

Bénir, 150.

Bercheure's translation of Livy, 39.

Boire, 150.

Bonheur, 175.

Bordeaux, school of, 4.

Bouclier, originally an adjective, 103.

Braire, 146.

Breton language, 6, 7.

Brunetto Latini wrote French, 17.

Burgundian French, 18.

Burgus, 7.